T0208404

SHANTISTAN

⌘ ENABLING ⌘
A Land of Peace

Ruth Vassar Burgess

WESTBOW
PRESS®
A DIVISION OF THOMAS NELSON
& ZONDERVAN

Copyright © 2020 Ruth Vassar Burgess.

All rights reserved. No part of this book may be used or reproduced by any means, graphic, electronic, or mechanical, including photocopying, recording, taping or by any information storage retrieval system without the written permission of the author except in the case of brief quotations embodied in critical articles and reviews.

This book is a work of non-fiction. Unless otherwise noted, the author and the publisher make no explicit guarantees as to the accuracy of the information contained in this book and in some cases, names of people and places have been altered to protect their privacy.

WestBow Press books may be ordered through booksellers or by contacting:

WestBow Press
A Division of Thomas Nelson & Zondervan
1663 Liberty Drive
Bloomington, IN 47403
www.westbowpress.com
844-714-3454

Because of the dynamic nature of the Internet, any web addresses or links contained in this book may have changed since publication and may no longer be valid. The views expressed in this work are solely those of the author and do not necessarily reflect the views of the publisher, and the publisher hereby disclaims any responsibility for them.

Any people depicted in stock imagery provided by Getty Images are models, and such images are being used for illustrative purposes only.
Certain stock imagery © Getty Images.

Cover created by Sophia Burgess

ISBN: 978-1-6642-0064-7 (sc)
ISBN: 978-1-6642-0065-4 (hc)
ISBN: 978-1-6642-0063-0 (e)

Library of Congress Control Number: 2020914046

Print information available on the last page.

WestBow Press rev. date: 12/09/2020

DEDICATION

Few persons find themselves cross-culturally astute and engrossed in history as Dr. Stanley Milton Burgess. It is only fitting that *Shantistan: Enabling a Land of Peace* be dedicated to this scholar. As a culture bearer, in the traditional sense, Stanley has positively marked his family, students and friends.

CONTENTS

INTRODUCTION: PEACEMAKING

Order

1. Narrative Themes
2. Culture Bearers
3. Mediated Learning Phases
4. Organization of Book
5. Collaboration Team

Understanding Similarities and Respecting Differences

Shantistan contains methods of peacemaking between antagonists whether they be religious, familial or between communities and nations.

Cultures are composed of narratives. Some reflect their heritage beliefs and practices. Other narratives emphasize mixed contemporary genres. The methods proposed by the sciences offer systematic ways of determining reality. Regardless of the transmission methods, narratives have the ability to shape one's reality. This influences the ability to learn as well as to shape individual and group identities. A group's sustainability requires its people of good will to work toward building a land of peace.

From the ancient language of Sanskrit the title is selected. "Shanti" refers to peace. "Stan" means land. The book's goal is achieved through understanding cultural similarities and respecting differences. Since the "understanding" is what enables *Shantistan* to extend heritage knowledge, to analyze contemporary understanding, and then to project peace-making into the future, we have both enabling processes and attainable goals.

In *Shantistan,* ideally three cross-cultural groups, who have received the "blessing" of their patriarch or leader, participate in peace making group exercises. The length of the workshop extends over several months, depending on their cultural time consideration. Participants gather and share cross cultural narratives that relate to the thirteen peace building themes. Each group understands they will replicate their training with other cross-cultural groups within an agreed time frame, thus becoming trainers-of-trainers. The trainers-of-trainers model will be used to extend *Shantistan.*

Shantistan seeks common understandings as expressed through life experience narratives. By reflecting on our religious and other cultural oral traditions, we identify stories illustrating peace-building themes. We come to recognize that there may be complementary heritage wisdom, personal experiences and education enculturation that support building a land of peace

Shantistan **Narrative Themes**
© Ruth Burgess 2020

In what ways are these themes communicated in your culture?
Did they evolve through (a) heritage beliefs and traditions or
(b) adopted from contemporary thoughts and practices?

Integrity
Harmony
Tolerance
Devotion to Beliefs
Love
Doing Good
Civility
Human Dignity
Brotherhood, Sisterhood, Humankind
Faith and Forgiveness
Protection of Life
Sacrifice
Reconciliation

Through the life experience narratives, problem solving approaches are studied. Participants recognize the benefits when one values multiple perspectives and show tolerance toward diverse ethnocentric beliefs. This tolerance can lead efforts to peace making. Conversely, egocentric actions pose opportunities for the teams to engage in thoughtful examples and ask for clarification through pertinent questions. One such question could be, "What are the long term effects to the individual as well as to the cultural groups who do not engage in peace making?"

These mediated and collaborative sorties provide the opportunity to lead participants to cognitive and affective flexibility and modifiability. There is an expanding need for these groups and the training of culture bearers since heritage values and wisdom principles seem to be held in less regard. Accelerated transportation opportunities and increasing access to technology have supported the loss of earlier memories of peace making. Now globally, we are faced with critical challenges. Who will put on the mantle of culture bearing?

Intergenerational transmission of stories is important. *How* and *who* listens to peace making creates **Shantistan.** Therefore, our thoughtful interactions with Life Experience stories are enhanced as we use mediated learning principles and collaborative consultation strategies during our interactions.

"Mediated learning is the interaction process between the developing human organism and an experienced adult, who by interposing himself between the student and external sources of stimulation, mediates the world to him by framing, selecting, focusing and feeding back environmental experience in such a way as to create appropriate learning sets." Reuven Feuerstein, © 1980, 2015

Mediated learning is not just a description of behavior, but a value statement and a belief system as well. There must be a commitment to enabling mediated interactions. This requires the formulation of intended outcomes, such as the development of self-regulated learners, who are capable of representational thinking, efficient problem solvers and decision makers, and effective co-mediation participants.

Collaborative Consultation recognizes the strength of cross-culture and cross-generation dialogues. These occur when two or more people cooperatively and systematically work for the good of others. There is the recognition that heritage, contemporary and scientific systems of thought and practice influence society. Each of these systems have knowledge, dispositions of the mind and dispositions of the spirit that are helpful in peace making. In **Shantistan,** teams participate in joint classroom activities to share cultural life experience stories that illustrate the peacemaking themes. Each collaborator is on equal footing in the collaborative process. Open communication with the different cultural groups is ongoing as the **Shantistan** participants learn to mediate in joint classroom activities, such as making collegial projects and participating in turn-about training opportunities.

Culture Bearers

The development of culture bearing is encouraged. Reading cross-cultural language experience stories that are focused on peace building themes stirs one's mind to seek peace building in one's culture. These culture bearers are committed to the survival and well- being of their knowledge, habitat and people. Their past, present and anticipated futures may be precarious if not carried forward.

Then as participants observe similarities or differences in the narratives, they have an opportunity to analyze multiple perspectives as to how people sought to make a land of peace. The following chart introduces culture bearing phases. Each phase captures the complexity of a culture bearer's responsibilities.

Culture Bearer's Mediated Learning Phases

Phase 1. Recognize the significance of one's values and place in human survival.

Phase 2. Believe in human modifiability, because we are created in the image of God.

Phase 3. Recognize one's role as a culture mediator and assume the responsibility to respect multiple perspectives when enabling positive alternatives.

Phase 4. Plan for a "fused horizon" between the cultural mediator and collaborators.

Phase 5. Continue to gain an understanding of heritage and experiential contexts.

Phase 6. Mediate or teach for process and intent within cultural contexts.

Phase 7. Reflect and extract values, wisdom principles or concepts from mediated encounters.

Phase 8. Extend, generalize and transpose transcendent values, wisdom principles or concepts in other contents and contexts.

Phase 9. Support the crystallization of the cognitive operations and processes through additional mediated encounters.

Phase 10. Encourage automatization of the cognitive operations and modalities by providing experiences with complexity, novelty and abstraction.

Phase 11. Become a mentor to a novice culture bearer, thus enabling a principled and reasoned future.

Organization for Presenting *Shantistan*

As a workbook that contains theory and practical application, both approaches are placed one after the other. For example, **Basic Information** is presented first and followed by **Supplement A: Communication Assistance**, which contains application suggestions.

Section One: Searching for *Shantistan* introduces a procedure suggested for group interactions. Then a completed example using a lesson on an "Integrity life lesson" is presented. Use of the quote boxes are provided as examples appropriate for individual differences. **Supplement B: Multiple Perspectives** provides varied creative application examples.

Section Two: *Shantistan* Peace Narratives presents thirteen peace-making narrative examples as well as a chart for the collaborators to record their life experience stories. The student narrative forms are in **Supplement C:** Narrative Forms Applied.

Section Three: Heritage Experiences suggests using the Heritage Box exercise as a way of furthering understanding within and among *Shantistan* participants. Other progressive peace building possibilities are in **Supplement D: Extending *Shantistan*.**

This book is based on and reflects the author's years of experience as a trainer-of-trainers, both in academic and culturally diverse settings.

Collaboration Team

The following materials are reprinted with permission. They were selected based on the themes of **Shantistan**. These cross-cultural stories and artwork are placed across times, situations and places. An attempt was made to maintain a range of perspectives, rather than simply present a single western view.

Anonymous. The Quest. 1991. Center for Research and Service. Burgess Archives

Burgess, David. 1985. Two Poem Narratives. Burgess Archives.

Chang, Edward, 1991. Comment. Center for Research and Service. Missouri State University.

Dodson, Elizabeth. 2019. **Shantistan** Quilt. Burgess Archives.

Feuerstein, Reuven, et al. 2015. *Changing Minds & Brains-the Legacy of Reuven Feuerstein. Higher Thinking & Cognition Through Mediated Learning.* New York: Teacher College Press. Columbia, University.

Kagarise, Robbie. 2010. Two Narratives. Burgess Archives.

Kolodiejchuk, MC, Director. One Narrative, Mother Teresa Center.

Luckert, Karl. 2009. Definition. Department of Religious Studies. Missouri State University. Burgess Archives.

Ling Yi Lin, 1991. Comment. Center for Research and Service. Missouri State University.

Nicholos, Patricia. 2010. Narrative. Burgess Archives.

Nixon, Carolyn Brown. 1991, 1992. Two Poem Narratives. Burgess Archives.

Richardson, Mark. 1991. Poem. Burgess Archives.

Turner, Richard. 1991. Comment. Center for Research and Service. Missouri State University.

Waschick, Kory. 2020. Graphics and Diagrams. Center for Research and Service, Burgess Archives.

Supplement A

Communication Assistance

Depending on the student's heritage background, contemporary experiences and the teacher's goals, the following exercises can assist enabling a variety of communication acts. This flexible approach creates a curriculum developing in process and one that is adaptable to cross-cultural understandings.

1. Acrostics: this exercise promotes socialization and communication.
2. Selected Mediated Reciprocity Encounters: encourages metacognition and dispositions of the mind.
3. When I …: reviews personal habits of the mind.
4. My Heritage Culture: proposes personal examples from one's heritage culture.
5. **Shantistan** and Similes I, II.: provides practice in an alternate form of thinking.
6. **Shantistan** and Negative Similes: mental flexibility using curriculum vocabulary are represented.
7. Opposites: supports communication flexibility.

SHANTISTAN ACROSTICS

Ruth Burgess. © 2020

Acrostics assist in vocabulary building. Building an Acrostic assists in creating common vocabulary. Also, encourage participants to prepare Acrostics in another language.

Preparation

One, select an appropriate word that relates to. ("key word")

Two, write one letter from the word vertically.

Three, think of other words that begin with the same letter to be the key word and write it by the example. Four, lead the group in a discussion about the significance of word study.

EXAMPLES

S	saga		**C**	covenant
H	heritage		**U**	undaunted
A	acceptance		**L**	loyal
N	noteworthy		**T**	transcendent
T	tolerance		**U**	universal
I	integrity		**R**	reflect
S	spiritual		**E**	earnest
T	think		**B**	brotherhood
A	accomplish		**E**	elegant
N	negotiate		**A**	acceptance
			R	reason
			E	empathy
			R	reconciliation

Selected Mediated Reciprocity Encounters
Ruth Burgess, © 2005

Instructions: In the spaces below, identify who mediated these cognitive functions for you? Why did they invest in you?

1. To focus your mind	**2. To "think-along" with others**
3. To treasure transcendent values & principles	**4. To value time concepts**
5. To use spatial cues	**6. To balance constancy & change**
7. To control impulsivity (both mental and physical)	**8. To respect multiple perspectives**
9. To believe you are mentally competent	**10. To appreciate challenges, novelties, & abstractions**

In what ways have you transmitted these cognitive functions in your context?

When I...
Ruth Burgess, © 2003

<u>Directions:</u> Read each of the sentence starters, think how you manage that thinking activity. Then complete each sentence.

1. When I try to understand an idea, I

   _____

2. When I am not sure of the meaning of a word, I

   _____

3. When I am asked to extend an idea beyond the current discussion, I

   _____

4. When I choose to do something different than my group, I

   _____

5. When I need to make goals, I

   _____

6. When I am confronted with a complex task or problem, I

   _____

7. When I monitor continual changes in myself, I

   _____

8. When I suggest positive alternatives through reasoned behavior, I

_____

9. When I regulate or control my behavior by "thinking about my thinking," I

_____

10. When I regard myself as a competent thinker and problem solver, I

_____

11. When I am asked to share a strategy or a reasoned insight, I

_____

12. When I am asked to focus my thoughts, I

_____

13. When I am told to be more systematic, I

_____

14. When I want someone to interact meaningfully with me, I

_____

15. When I question "why" an activity is important, I am seeking

_____

My Heritage Culture

R. Burgess. © 1992

Task: Give examples from your heritage culture pertaining to the following descriptors.

1. TIME concepts were

2. Self-identity was determined by

3. Meaning for living was established by

4. The place of "metaphoric learning" was

5. Questioning was

6. The approaches to problem solving used were

7. The value of multiple perspectives taking was

8. Survival was interpreted as

9. Change was seen as

10. The place of the child was

11. Rituals observed were

12. Stereotypic behavior was

13. Space meant

14. Ethnicity was

Shantistan and Similes (I)
Ruth Burgess. © 2013

A. Complete the following sentences. ***Shantistan*** is like ...

1. ...A river,   because

2. ...A mirror,   because

3. ...A butterfly,   because

4. ...A computer,   because

5. ...A minstrel,   because

6. ...Chaos & cosmos,   because

7. ...A right angle,   because

8. ...Swimming,   because

9. ...A patchwork quilt, because

B. Below draw a "metaphor" that illustrates ***Shantistan.***

Shantistan and Similes (II)
Ruth Burgess. © 2013

A. *Shantistan* is like ...

1. ...Clowning,   because

2. ...Fence building,   because

3. ...Popcorn,   because

4. ...Humpty Dumpty,   because

5. ...Preening,   because

6. ...Bubonic plague,   because

7. ...Cheerleaders,   because

8. ... Paper tissues,   because

9. ...Cyber-crime,   because

B. Describe the differences between a "simile" and a "metaphor."

OPPOSITES

Ruth Burgess. © 2005

Directions: Write the opposite word and give examples for each of the peace building themes. Avoid using a negative (not, no, ...) word or morph (i.e. un-, dis-, ...) when writing the opposite words.

The opposite of ...is ...

1. integrity   is _____

2. harmony   is _____

3. tolerance   is _____

4. devotion to beliefs   is _____

5. love   is _____

6. doing good   is _____

7. civility   is _____

8. human dignity   is _____

9. brotherhood / sisterhood   is _____

10. faith and forgiveness   is _____

11. protection of life   is _____

12. sacrifice   is _____

13. reconciliation   is _____

SECTION ONE

Searching for Shantistan

1. Early Cultural Formation
2. Dialogue: A Peace Building Process
3. Application: Case Study 2005
4. Shifts in Meaning Example

Understanding one's cultural traditions helps by participating in a variety of dialogues.

1. Social dialogues: where individuals work on common projects
2. Consultation: encourages making decisions using collaborative consultation phases
3. Lived experiences: draws on personal experiences
4. Historic experiences: seeks understanding and resolution of misunderstandings
5. Supportive dialogues: encourages groups of people to use mediation, as well as to plan and facilitate other dialogues

"

Kushtum (this is the problem)!
Ahmchee (mine) or thumchee (yours)?
In our relationship, do we have ...
"evolving meanings?"
"shared meanings?"
"disparate meanings?"
"mutual meanings?"
In what manner can we civilly affect our future?
Might interactive, focused mediation
provide a resolution?

Ruth Burgess. © 2016

Religion can encourage peace making or religious practices can obliterate life and decimate the land. Religion is a belief system to which one "bows his head and bends his knees." Karl Luckert

Shantistan is a social enhancement curriculum that blends heritage ways, contemporary beliefs and reasoned practices that lead one to participate in searching for and enabling a land of peace. Through gathering and sharing life experience relating to peace-making themes, one can better understand similarities and differences of interpretation over time and space. By using dialogue and mediated learning interactions, that support learning-to-learn strategies, both cognitive, social and affective growth is possible. These respectful approaches provide an alternative to single minded, doctoral approaches that require submission as contrasted to collaboration.

The loss of lives as well as the decimation of cultures and land requires us to engage in understanding each other's narratives and ways of making meanings ("ethnologic"). This includes respecting peace-building themes such as those presented in **Shantistan** (integrity, harmony, tolerance, devotion to beliefs, love, doing good, civility, human dignity, brotherhood and sisterhood, faith and forgiveness, protection of sacrifice and reconciliation.) In the pilot study (1995), we sought to gather and share peace building narratives from different religions (Hindu, Christian and Islam).

Respecting cross-culture practices, the leaders of their religious persuasion had recommended participants to participate on each of the three teams. We were hoping for cross-age, community respect and gender participation for team members.

In this section we provide additional background about **Shantistan.** Then the use of dialogue as a peace-making process is discussed. This leads to how mediated learning provided a grid for cognitive, social and affective changes. Peace-making narrative examples illustrate how these may apply to the *Shantistan* peace-making concepts, often cross-culturally. Ahmedabad, Gujarat, India provided insights for this pilot study.

❝

Global Bond

Liang Yi Lin. © 1991

"Education is a process of learning to become a matured person. It is not merely through knowledge acquisition, but also critical thinking, and interaction with ones surroundings at a global level. The core characteristics, which compose the matured personality, are universal, not just culture specific. The exercise of these characteristics, reflected upon a person's thinking process and behavior, is recognizable even in very different cultural contexts."

13

Shantistan (seeking "the land of peace") emerges as individuals and groups become culture bearers of minds and actions dedicated to peace-building. They sustain peaceful habits of the mind and spirit. Peace-building includes establishing a vision with goals that relate to creating and sustaining peaceful ways. From these steps, the peacemakers support the vision embodied in the Shantistan philosophy and curriculum.

The Quest
Anonymous, 1991

It is incumbent upon us to approach the agora as a place in which each person accepts responsibility for the meanings of the information that is transferred. The mediator must bring to the learning arena an inquiring spirit and a concern for learning. This calls to approach issues in an open and thoughtful way. This is the cognition that both individual identity and group identities are forming cognitive modifiability.

Four central elements are basic to this curriculum:

First, humans seeking a land of peace appreciate commonalities as well as unique characteristics among cultures.

Second, through understanding historical (temporal and spatial relations) precedence, one recognizes that different groups have adopted varying ways of understanding as well as making meanings ("ethnologic").

Three, through dialogue we seek understandings using the approach called the "mediated learning process."

Finally, collaborators analyze cultural ways through higher order thinking processes, rather than responding impulsively or reactively.

＂

A Philosopher
Euripides, 3rd and 4th BCE, Phoenissae

If all defined 'honorable' and 'wise' alike there would be no debate on earth. As it is, each man defines these words for himself, and only the names remain unchanged

What might we have in common? Symbolism. Through reasoned and principled behavior we have the opportunity to identify symbols that will sustain **Shantistan's** philosophy. We have been blessed with life and experiences that can be told and retold as stories containing symbols. These Life as Authoring narratives define and refine our understandings of reality. Heritage stories strengthen our self-identities, self-worth and group identities. Life experiences heard by others define our self-concepts. Whereas the narratives learned in academia usually assist us when using the scientific methods that support academic disciplines of learning, so it is advantageous to study the use of symbolism, regardless of the presentation manner.

In the **Shantistan** curriculum participants are encouraged to reflect on their life as an authoring experience. They identify and record narratives based on each one's heritage or tradition, other's experience and from scientific sources. Each narrative represents a core curricular theme (integrity, harmony, tolerance, devotion to beliefs, love, doing good, civility, human dignity, brotherhood or sisterhood, faith and forgiveness, protection of life, sacrifice and reconciliation).

This project highlights the significance of ethnologic when one engages in peacebuilding. Ethnologic or how one makes meanings is based on heritage and historical precedence. It is a recognition that often cultures strive to perpetuate their briefs through formal and informal folkways. When trying to understand others' perspectives, one will encourage the use of respectful interview strategies. Understanding others is a process that recognizes both alternate processes and multiple meanings. Participants withhold judgment until the logic is understood. Through our interchanges we must remember that peace building is our mission. Thus it becomes imperative to maintain clear communication with the cross-cultural communities that support the **Shantistan** participants.

Early Cultural Formations

Come with me and meet three families who have started cultural transmission with their three year olds. In the first family, Grandfather Gerrit Berghuis, the first generation born in the United States, sits as patriarch in his western Michigan home. Since many of the area residents immigrated from the Netherlands, it is common to hear the phrase, "You're not much, if you aren't Dutch." The second vignette records an interaction with residents in the United States. The family's ancestral home is in Taiwan.

The third pericope records a diatribe between a mother, her three year old son, and family members in Texas. This family would be classified as "old American stock."

Vignette One: Such were the Dutch

As was the weekly practice, each of the Gerrit Berghuis' three daughters and his two sons with their families brought a covered dish for a Sunday afternoon meal. Grandfather along with sons and son-in-law sat watching the cloudy television screen looking for a commentary about the Friday evening boxing bonanza. Suggestions as to how to tilt the rabbit ears antenna, moving the set, or the price reductions of the new colored sets was offered. Three grandsons and a granddaughter were laughing and skipping through doorways that made a circular pathway. Stanley kept his right hand in his bulging suit pants when Aunt Lydia announced lunch was on the table.

Gerrit invited the men to accompany him to the table. Then the women and children filled in the spaces between their men. With heads bowed in a reverent manner, the aged voice thanked God for food and family. A rush of breath caught the smells and colors. The anticipation rose that perhaps today the ever present Jell-O mold would slip off the platter. Then one of the cousins took the contents out of his pocket. It was a new red, metal Buick toy. "Hey, Stanley, here catch it. I'll roll it across the table."

Stanley squealed high anticipating catching the toy car. Then, in a thunderous voice Gerrit proclaimed, "How many times have I told you that a child must be seen, but not heard!"

Johannes quickly apologized for his son's behavior and took away the toy. Francie scolded Stanley for not remembering the rules. Frederick told Stanley he didn't have to do what his cousin wanted him to do. Stanley looked at the food dished on his plate and his stomach bunched up like a hard turnip.

Vignette Two: Encouraging Trust

The Chang family, Edward, Liang and Felix, were visiting at a friend's house. On a low lying table in front of Edward and Felix was a brightly painted paper cache box. Felix began to look at the box and then gazed at his father. Several times the three-yearold did this. Picking up on Felix' interest Edward said, "Felix, would you like to look at the box?"

The child stared but gave no facial expression. Again Edward said, "Felix would you like to look at the box with me?" Felix gave a small nod. Edward sat on the floor beside Felix, reached over the box, picked it up and brought it close to his son.

Felix looked, but made no movement nor changed his expression. The father put the box down on the table. Then, gently he took his son's hands and they both picked up the lacquered box and brought it to the edge of the table and admired it before putting it back in the original position. In the third interaction, Edward said, "Now, Felix you can reach over there and pick up the box on your own." This Felix did.

Vignette Three: Train Up a Child

There stands a bungalow made of rock and grey mortar just off Main Street in Seagraves, Texas. Off the hallway to the right and through glass French doors was the formal dining room. As was common in those times, several corners of a room might be used for displaying "what nots." Now, "what nots" could be any kind of collectible item, such as small china pitchers, baby ivory teething rings, glass thimbles, a Jim Bowie knife, over endowed porcelain Texas longhorn bulls, or metal replicas of the Golden Gate Bridge. Of course, some of these precious mementos were at eye level of preschool children. But keeping the artifacts in sight and in place was thought to be good for "teaching disciplines."

Papa and Mama had come for Sunday dinner. Seven-year-old Susan announced that her three-year-old brother, Johnny, was touching the "what nots" again. Eager to show Mama her good parenting skills, Tara rushed in and spanked Johnny's right hand. "How many times have I told you not to tough those things?" Johnny's blue eyes filled with tears. Turning to Susan, "How many times have I told you to watch him?" Tara started back to the kitchen to stir the chicken gravy when she heard, "Mother, he is doing it again." Turning back Tara spanked Johnny's hands again.

Papa standing between the French doors said, "You are doing right Tara. He has to learn right from wrong. He has to learn discipline."

What Values Were Being Transmitted?

The three vignettes illustrated different enculturation practices. The first and second vignettes carried child rearing beliefs from Europe and Asia; while the third vignette represented a mixture of American background traditions. All three had values they wished to transmit, but the first and third appear to be harsh. In the second vignette. Edward became a mediating elder. Felix learned thoughtfully through his father's modeling and sequential steps. The pair remained focused throughout the learning encounter. No evidence of shame and negative labeling occurred. Felix grew in his understanding that he was a capable learner and his father was a trustworthy mediator.

Positive learning-to-learn strategies were largely missing in Vignette One and Vignette Three. Gender roles were crystallized. Of course, the young grandchildren were expected to comply with the external adult authoritarian rules. The children's internal thoughts appeared as spontaneous reactions to environmental stimuli. Interestingly, the adult parents of the children appeared still under the authoritarian mindsets of the male leaders of their packs. Neither the adults nor the children used the occasion to support mental competence.

By taking Felix's perspective, Edward was able to create a learning situation that enhanced boding between the father and son. Psychological pain, such as public shame, occurred in Vignette One, while both physical and psychological pain occurred in Vignette Three. Foundations of anger, suppression of emotions and lack of positive learning-to-learn skills set in childhood have continuing effects.

Dialogue, a Peace-Building Process

Dialogue is the method of collective inquiry that seeks learning. The intent is to build common understandings in a collective manner and encourage a nonjudgmental situation. On the other hand mediated learning interchanges inquire into the thinking process that is behind or beneath an issue or action. With active reflective thinking the intent is to move from solely egocentric or ethnocentric thinking to mental flexibility that seeks common understandings. This promotes understanding - not an adoption of another's persuasion.

The following five steps are provided as guides to be used relating to cross-cultural understandings.

1. Awareness Step

    * Are the collaborators aware of historical and contemporary issues?
    * What are the possible implications to persons and community?
    * Who seems aware of different meta-praxis practices?

2. Metalogue, Metacognition, Metapraxis Step

    * Am I maintaining an internal thought discourse?
    * How am I thinking? (metacognition)
    * Am I reflecting through an "ethno-cultural lens?"
    * Which cultural mindset am I feeling, seeing, smelling or listening?

3. Inquiry Step

    * Am I suspending judgment while asking questions?
    * Am I using cross-culturally appropriate non-verbal and language patterns when generating and asking questions?
    * Do I plan a follow-up question for clarification purposes, if thought necessary?
    * Do I seek cross cultural vocabulary and concepts to bring clarity?
    * How is the interview format culturally appropriate?

4. Reflection Step

    * Am I reflecting with thoughtful deliberation?
    * Are we sharing the steps or the decision making process?
    * Are we exploring our thought processes?
    * Have we compared or contrasted similar perspectives?
    * Have we made clear that differences are not deficiencies?

5. Advocacy Step

* Have I planned how to present my position?
* Will I give reasoned support while being open to alternate opinion?
* Explain how your position addresses possible short term and longterm goals.

""

Appreciation for Positive Disequilibrium
Richard Turner. ©1991

*Years ago I had a teacher who said that true learning is a violent process -
new ideas revise or replace old beliefs, or they forge their own place. I like
to think of teaching as an opportunity to help a student grow intellectually,
as a result of exposure to the positive and creative violence of learning: a
chance to help them go beyond the comfortable and complacent, to examine
the new and challenging.*

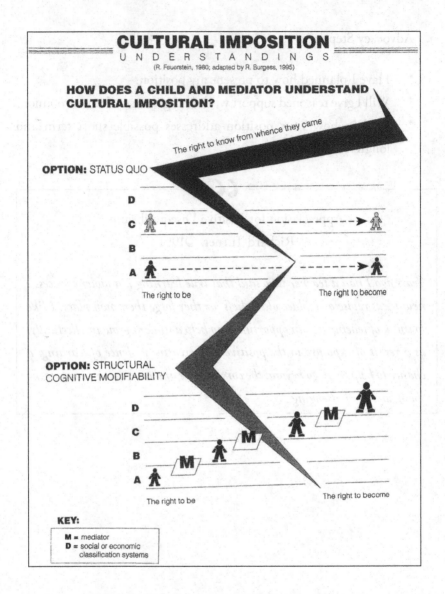

CULTURAL IMPOSITION
U N D E R S T A N D I N G S
(R. Feuerstein, 1980; adapted by R. Burgess, 1995)

HOW DOES A CHILD AND MEDIATOR UNDERSTAND CULTURAL IMPOSITION?

The right to know from whence they came

OPTION: STATUS QUO

The right to be   The right to become

OPTION: STRUCTURAL COGNITIVE MODIFIABILITY

The right to be   The right to become

KEY:
M = mediator
D = social or economic classification systems

Kory Waschick. 2020 Cultural Imposition

The graphic contrasts two models. In the Status Quo Model, people remain stuck with little hope for an alternative future. Whereas in the Structural Cognitive Modifiability Model, people continue to have an alternative for change through mediated cognitive modifiability experiences.

Applications: Case Study 2005

Cross-cultural pathways were noted in Case Study 2005. First, there was the recognition that there may be different stages apparent among people of similar kin. The first group of trainer-of-trainers were brave, intelligent and able to make change in their environments. They should be applauded for their desire to seek peace-making in their diverse communities.

Ahmedabad, India provided the site for a field application of *Shantistan* (2005). This sprawling city experienced trauma when 2,000 Hindus and Muslims were killed over issues relating to sacred space and time. Case Study 2005

"

We understood similarities and respected differences within our evolving cultural contexts.

Ruth Burgess. © 2017

A team from three religions (Christianity, Hinduism and Islam) volunteered to participate in the mediated learning pilot study. Before the cross- cultural trainer of trainers were selected, *Shantistan* curricular leaders thought to make and strengthen the trust with the targeted three religious groups. It was seen as a novel curriculum entitled *Shantistan*. The training occurred over six weeks and the three teams met three times per week. Success of this encounter was articulated to mean that the inter-religious team would replicate the curriculum at a high school where there were teachers and students who had a variety of religious beliefs. (At first, I was unsure if they would be able to implement the course.)

First, communications reflecting trust building as well as sharing the *Shantistan* goals were discussed with the respected community elders. It is from these respected cultural communities that the elders then deleted their participants. Who would participate in this peace-building project? Occasionally these small groups reported back to their elders sharing their impressions relating to the Shantistan goals and our progress.

Three elements confirmed how teamwork was progressing. This included interactions, relationships and interdependence. Early in the process roles and responsibilities were clarified. Shared leadership roles were encouraged. At the close of each class the students recorded in their log what they had learned that evening. Discussions included how different government and ethnic groups managed recent conflicts. The group shared feelings that included fears and concerns. All the while we built trust among ourselves.

An evening supporting peacemaking we learned from one another.
Burgess archive
Participants: Dolly Bhat, Roma Rajan, Henry
Christian, Shabana and Mr. Saikh

Communication proved to be a challenge since the participants had different levels of proficiency in Hindi, Punjabi, Marathi, Arabic, English and Urdu. In the long run, these differences provided an opportunity to slow down the rate of instruction. The students became interpreters for one another. This accelerated the stages of growth among the team. Differences in decision-making, both in their communities and in the classroom discussions, began to be noticed. As a result, shared responsibility for presenting their narratives as well as making plans for replicating the workshop occurred. Each brought different resources that included different skills and contacts that strengthened the team.

Besides the cultural narrative dialogues, the group enjoyed "chai and biscuits" provided by the director of Shanti Ashram. Social activities during the break times included some language extension activities. Some of these activities included the following:

* discussing the Golden Rule in eight traditions,
* preparing two *Shantistan* Acronym charts in English and Hindi,
* developing a Metacognition Acrostic,
* developing an Opposites chart relating to the Peace-building themes and
* suggesting similes that support *Shantistan* themes.

The Shifts in Meaning exercise assisted in understanding differences. This is the first exercise illustrating changes in meaning. It assesses different personal interpretations and extracting a possible transcendent value (TV) or wisdom saying (WS). This meaning should be accurate beyond time, place, circumstance, person and situation.

Shifts in Meanings

Instructions: Each collaborator selects a Life Experience Story from prepared cards. At this point the story is not discussed with the others.

After reading your colleague's story, first write the title of the story and then write your name on the line below. On 1.1 paraphrase your understanding (basic meaning) in three sentences or less. Then on 1.2 write a more abstract value relating to the story. Fold the exercise sheet on the dotted line. Each member hands his or her sheet to the right and each person completes the same information as above.

Title of Story:

Reader #1:

1.1 (Paraphrase the story)

1.2 (Write a transcendent value or Wisdom Principle relating to the story.)

---------------Please fold and give it to your collaborator---------------

Reader #2:

2.1 (Paraphrase the story)

2.2 (Write a Transcendent Value or Wisdom Principle relating to the story.)

Afterwards each team reads and analyzes the similarities or differences in interpretation.

Why are there differences regarding the same materials?

Now we integrate the first *Shantistan* Peace Theme with a Heritage Value. (Integrity)

I. INTEGRITY
My Father, a Righteous Man
Patricia A. Nicholas. © 2008

Integrity is the first peace-building theme. Family stories from our youth help mold our future. Dr. Patricia A. Nicholas shares such a life lesson from her teen-age years.

I. Life Narrative Example (1.1)

Nicholas's father required his daughter to return an ashtray, which brought temporary embarrassment. In the long run, this life lesson stood her well. First, read her story and think about the meaning. Second, enter into a conversation with your collaborator.

Shantistan Theme: Integrity

Patricia A. Nicholas

Back in the old days when I was a teenager the popular thing to do was to go to a drive-in eating-place to finish off a date.

One night my boyfriend and I joined several others at such a place called Rustins. The waitress brought out our tray of food plus an ash tray with "Rustins" painted on it. It was a nice keepsake serving as a reminder of a wonderful time with my friends. So I took it home and put it on my dresser.

My dad came into my bedroom to tell me good night and saw the ashtray. He asked me how I got it and why I wanted it since I did not smoke. I explained that everyone took ashtrays as reminders of the good times they had at a particular place.

Well, my dad said that I was to get up out of bed, dress, and go with him. Of course, I did. He drove me back to Rustins. When we arrived Dad handed me the ashtray. I was to take it in and tell the manager that I had taken it and was now returning it, as it was not mine.

The lesson was well learned and to this day never forgotten.

2. Example of The *Shantistan* Process

Shantistan Meaning Shifts

I. Hand out *a **Shantistan*** Themes Narrative to partner groups.

II. Write the title of a Peace-building narrative: *An Integrity Lesson*

Write your name in this Reader #1 space: Abe

Reader # 1. After reading the Peace-building narrative, paraphrase your understanding (basic meaning) in 3 sentences or less. *A father teaches a lifelong lesson.*

Reader #1 Then write a more abstract meaning (transcendent value or wisdom principle) that is important beyond the current place, time, person or circumstance that relates to the Peace-building narrative. *Love and care extends beyond money.*

III. Please fold and give this paper to Reader #2, who writes their name, but does not read Reader # 1 comments.

-------------------------------please fold-----------------------------

IV. Write your name as Reader #2 on your partner's paper: Eve

Reader #2 reads the narrative and writes a brief paraphrase of the story. *Why were there no guardians with the teenagers?*

Reader #2 extracts and writes a transcendent value or wisdom principle. *"Birds of a feather should flock together."*

V. Group Understanding. The completed **_Shantistan_** Meaning Shifts papers are returned to their first writer and a group discourse follows.

3. Conversations with my partner and group collaborators.

After reading the narrative, complete the following exercise. This is an opportunity to share and collaborate.

a.   Define Integrity as you read your collaborator's paper.
b.   Briefly write a synopsis of the story's lesson on Integrity.
c.   In what ways does this Life Narrative illustrate Integrity?
d.   Explain why Integrity is relevant when one is peace-building.
e.   Now, consider ethnologic reflections. From past experiences, identify the ways your associate's understandings are alike or different from yours. Make a check mark in the column that describes your thoughts.

	same	similar	different	other
definition				
narrative example				
applies to peacemaking				
cultural influences				

4. Questions I would like to ask of my associate.
5. Write a transcendent value or wisdom principle that can be extracted from this lesson.

Name: _____

Date _____

Reflections

As the Shanti sessions are coming to a close, I ask the group to "think along with me" about these recent experiences. Eleven comments guided the discussion.

1. When did everyone realize that each person had something significant to share?

   _____

2. At what point was everyone in the group learning together?

   _____

3. In what ways did multiple perspectives help in the search for meanings?

   _____

4. How do wisdom principles or transcendent values assist in developing representational thought?

   _____

5. Why is a willingness or an orientation-to-learn necessary for positive decision making?

   _____

6. Explain what happens when you regulate and reflect on your thinking? (metacognition or metapraxis)

   _____

7. Give examples when individual and group identities may cause positive or negative disequilibrium.

_____

8. In what ways does the feeling of belonging assist in learning?

_____

9. Explain the importance of maintaining an optimistic outlook?

_____

10. In what ways can humans change or remain the same?

_____

Listening Here

Listening here, today
I have been each of you and
Another and
My family, also.
Who am I now, then?
I am each of you, as your
Speech creates me.
I am another, as my
Hearing destroys me.
And I am my family, also,
As I assume the quiet
Mind of my ancestors.

Mark Richardson. © 2-16-1991

Supplement B

Multiple Perspectives

The following graphics and poem are enrichment materials for the teacher/ mediator. When one integrates varied cognitive modalities, a strengthening of cognition and social behavior occurs. Peace making can occur as one learns multiple ways of understanding life.

1. Culture Bearer Graphic: Explain the significance of culture bearing.
2. RIP: Multiple perceptions: Contrast two different understandings. (Christian "Rest in Peace," Hindu "Return if Possible")
3. Search for Understandings: "Think along" exercise.
4. Hutee (elephant) Misperceptions: Location influences multi perceptions.
5. Orientation in Space: What makes the front of a pumpkin?
6. Birds: You and Birds: What is the story behind the two circles in the center?
7. The Piece in the Center: Poem, discuss #6 and #7 together.
8. Two Perceptions: Cognitive Differences influences culture.
9. Towards Understanding: Bridging the Gap.
10. Purposeful Questions # 1: Communication and cognitive goals.
11. Purposeful Questions # 2: Cultural goals.

Culture Bearer
Ruth Burgess. © 2000

What does it mean to be a Culture Bearer (külterbearer)?

_____

_____

_____

_____

_____

Two Cultural Perspectives
Ruth Burgess. © 2020

As an investigating reporter explain the narratives in the graphic.

In Search of Understandings...
Crucial Question

How can human beings maintain their heritage identity but learn more constructive orientations toward those outside their group?

R. Burgess. © 2020

Positive Examples

Types of Examples	People Involved	Time Period	How did it happen?
1.			
2.			

Perspectives on an Elephant

How do perspectives affect one's vision?

1. Left rear perspective

2. Front side view

3. Right side view

4. Rear side

5. Ant on floor looking up

6. Mosquito's viewpoint from above

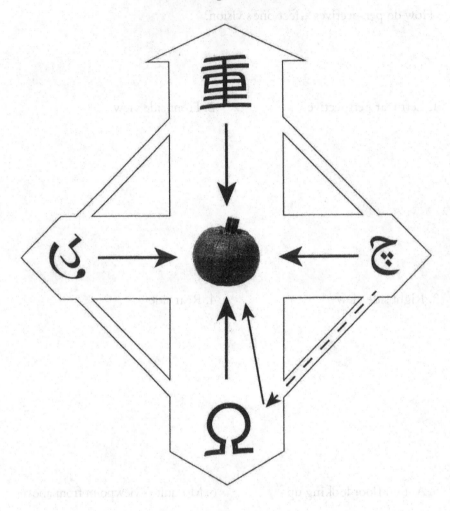

MULTIPLE PERSPECTIVES FROM A DISTANCE
Ruth Burgess ©1990

What are their perspectives? How did they come to practice that perspective?

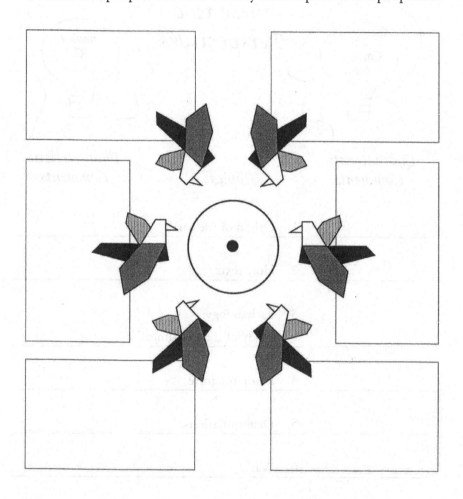

Two Truths: Which One is Correct?

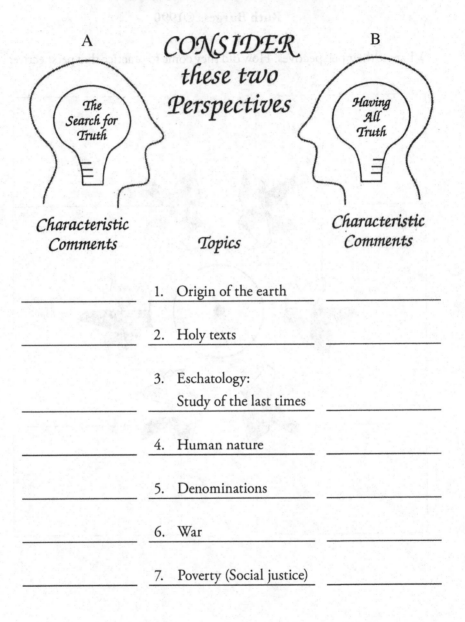

A

CONSIDER
these two
Perspectives

B

The
Search for
Truth

Having
All
Truth

Characteristic
Comments

Topics

Characteristic
Comments

_____   1. Origin of the earth   _____

_____   2. Holy texts   _____

_____   3. Eschatology:
                        Study of the last times   _____

_____   4. Human nature   _____

_____   5. Denominations   _____

_____   6. War   _____

_____   7. Poverty (Social justice)   _____

Ruth Burgess ©2000

Towards Understandings

R. Burgess ©1995

What does my community believe about _____?
(Issue)

Is there more than one perspective? What are they?

A _____ _____ B

_____ _____

_____ _____

_____ _____

_____ _____

Backgrounds or historical legacies behind these perspectives:

A _____

_____

_____

B _____

_____

_____

Purposeful Questions - 1
Ruth Burgess © 2005

Instructions: The facility of posing purposeful questions is a fine art. In column 1 are some communication goals. These relate to different cognitive and communication goals. In column 2, you are to write questions that fulfill the communication goals. Do not use the words in column 1 as part of your question. In column 3, identify the question types (i.e. narrow based, broad based recall, comprehension, application, analysis, synthesis, evaluation, ...)

Goals	Write questions below.	Question types
1. seek information		
2. check understanding		
3. propose a definition		
4. explain thought process		
5. determine relevance		

6. paraphrase an instruction		
7. translate into formal language use		
8. inquire about belief (-s)		
9. inquire about thought process		
10. translate into informal language use		

Three things I learned from this exercise are:

1.

2.

3.

Purposeful Questions - 2
Ruth Burgess © 2005

<u>Instructions:</u> Posing purposeful questions takes practice. In column 1 are some communication goals. These relate to different cognitive and communication goals. In column 2, you are to write questions that fulfill these communication goals. Do not use the words in column 1 as part of your question. In column 3, identify the question types (i.e. broad based recall, comprehension, application, analysis, synthesis, evaluation, divergent, justification, reconstruct, hypothesize, value ...)

Goals	Write questions below.	Question types
1. **predict or infer an ending to a story**		
2. **judge the accuracy of a translation**		
3. **defend a cultural value**		
4. **reconstruct a misinformed policy**		
5. **hypothesize rationales for miscues**		

6. contrast gender interpretations		
7. appraise the value of inquiry		
8. defend the use of critique		
9. simulate the outcomes of the Apostle's Creed		
10. subdivide different research approaches		

Something I learned from this exercise is:

*Suggestion: Use this poem just after the BIRDS – MULTIPLE PERSPECTIVES ON PAGE 39 ...

The Piece in the Center

I am the piece in the center;

The universe revolves around me.

I am the piece in the center;

The universe resides within me.

I am but a piece of the center;

Pieces of the center are within me. (paragraph break)

As I contemplate ...

Wholeness and partness disintegrate

Melt away and gravitate

Wholeness and partness disintegrate

Melt away and gravitate ...

Wholeness and partness await ...

Suspended in time which I can no longer separate. (paragraph break)

I am the piece in the center;

The past lies within me – behind me.

I am the piece in the center;

The present lies within me – enshrouds me.

I am the piece in the center;

The future lies within me – awaits me. (paragraph break)

I am the piece in the center,

The past, the present, the future,

The fusion of time and space.

I am the Piece in the Center.

Carolyn B. Nixon. © September 1, 1991

SECTION TWO

Shantistan Peace Narratives

A. Introduction

B. *Shantistan* Quilt Blocks

C. Mediated Learning Probes

D. Questions

E. *Shantistan* Process

F. *Shantistan* Narratives

    1. Lesson on "Integrity"

    2. "Mud in Your Eyes"

    3. "Bloods All Red"

    4. "Where Has It Gone?"

    5. "Love"

    6. "Mother Teresa"

    7. "Maria of Chicago"

    8. "Pomp and Ceremony"

    9. "The Man on the Street"

    10. "The Favorite Son"

    11. "Ahmedabad is Burning"

    12. "All for a Son"

    13. "The Peacemaker"

G. Inventory of Life Experience Stories, form

SHANTISTAN NARRATIVES
Introduction.

As this project evolved, we searched for a pictorial image that embodied the *Shantistan* components. This emblem was to represent three types of goals: a. identity, b. relational, and task relationships. This image was to have cross-cultural examples. Some of the inherent characteristics would be to exhibit comfort, warmth, beauty, preservation, artwork, culture bearing, support bonding, protection, provide funds, as well as encourage individual and group identities. Yes, this pictorial emblem became the *Shantistan* Quilt.

The *Shantistan* quilt blocks are built on thirteen peace-building themes. This heritage quilt illustrates each of these peace-making narratives. It is interesting that the Reconciliation Quilt block encompasses the other twelve quilt blocks with joined hands. The artwork was designed and quilted by Elizabeth Dotson (2019). These illustrations serve as well as possible examples for other stories.

There will be differences in the interpretation of these visuals that are worthy of seeking clarity. After analyzing these examples, the participants are encouraged to seek similar experience stories and quilt blocks from their culture. Thereby relevant curriculum is formed around these culturally sensitive central concepts and life stories.

In *Shantistan* participants share life experiences relating to the peace-building themes. These culturally diverse stories encourage others to become culture bearers, who promote peaceful interactions. Through explicit interactions participants are encouraged to develop cognitive and social modifiability, to recognize strength in multiple perspectives and to encourage the use of metacognition.

Shantistan life narratives detail human experiences. Participants share life oriented narratives based on peace-building themes. These are not historical records, but serve as a memoir of life's hopeful search for peacemaking. Our intent is to share this authenticity. The varied levels of interpretation rely on cross-cultural and heritage sensitive culture bearers, who enable peaceful interactions.

Peace Narratives Quilt Blocks

1. "Lesson on Intergrty

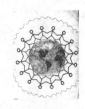

2. "Mud in Your Eyes"

3. "Blood's All Red"

4. "Where Has It Gone"

5. "Love"

6. "Mother Teresa"

7. "Maria of Chicago"

8. "Pomp and Ceremony"

9. "The Man on
the Street"

10. "The Favorite Son

11. "Ahmedabad
is Burning"

12. "All for a Son"

13. "The Peacemaker"

Quilt Blocks created by
Elizabeth Dodson. © 2019

SECTION II *Shantistan* Narratives

1. "Lesson on Integrity," Patricia Nicholas, (Integrity), see Section I
2. "Here is Mud in Your Eye," Robbie Kagarise, (Harmony)
3. "Bloods All Red," David Burgess, (Tolerance)
4. "Where Has It Gone?", David Burgess, (Devotion to Belief)
5. "Tough Love," Ruth V. Burgess, (Love)
6. "Mother Teresa," Mother Teresa Center," (Doing Good)
7. "Marla of Chicago," Ruth V. Burgess, (Civility)
8. "Pomp and Ceremony," Ruth V. Burgess, (Human Dignity)
9. "The Man on the Street," Robbie Kargarise, (Human Kind)
10. "The Favorite Son," Ruth V. Burgess, (Faith and Forgiveness)
11. "Ahmedabad is Burning," Ruth V. Burgess, (Protection of Life)
12. "All for a Son," Ruth V. Burgess, (Sacrifice)
13. "The Peace-maker," Fifteenth Century India Legend, (Reconciliation)
14. Tracking Sheet for *Shantistan* theme stories.

These life experience narratives are disclosures detailing human experiences. The intention is to share authenticity cross-culturally. These are not historical records, but serve as memoirs of life's hopeful search for peace-making.

51

Enabling Growth Through Questions

Questions may be in the form of a gesture, word, phrase or sentence. Questions are a means of extending one's knowledge, and challenging dispositions of the mind and spirit. Five types of questions are presented: metacognitive types, broad based questions, narrow based questions, Socratic questioning and mediated learning questions.

1. Questions may promote the use of metacognition, metapraxis and the regulation of mental behavior. These questions require the student to retrace his thoughts to determine the origin or process used in his answer. These insights can assist in future decisions.

2. Broad based questions simulate divergent and evaluate thought approaches. Example of divergent cognitive functions are prediction, hypothesize, inference, and reconstruction.

3. Narrow based questions tap cognitive memory and convergent (systematic inquiry) thought. Example relating to memory are recall, identify, yes/no answers, define, name and designate. Examples of systematic inquiry include explanations, state relationships, compare and contract phenomenon and analogical thinking.

4. Socratic questions elicits and probes student through by raising and pursuing basic problematic issues. Collaborators ask students to slow their thinking, elaborate on it and to reflect on it.

5. Mediated learning addresses dispositions of the mind and spirit. Habits of the mind include self-regulation and control of mental behavior, goal setting, extracting or educing transcendent values and wisdom principles, organizing and recognizing multiple perspectives. Some examples of Habits of the Spirit include a sense of belonging, search for positive alternatives, feelings of mental competence, positive anticipating challenging, willingness to share on different levels, showing culturally and context appropriate respects.

Shantistan Life Narratives' Process

The **Shantistan** Life as Narratives' Process was developed to illustrate that interpretations may be altered, even when using the same stimuli. This may occur due to different heritage understandings, loss of sensory acuteness such as hearing or vision loss, or even altered experience and resources.

Shantistan Process
Ruth Burgess. © 2000

Step One: Mediator introduces the Life as Experience Narratives to the group. These stories are built around peace themes in different times and cultures. Because they are chosen purposefully from different contexts, the initial reactions may differ. "Difference does not mean deficiency." Dyads are formed.

Step Two: Individuals read and complete the first narrative worksheet.

Step Three: Collaborators exchange papers. They read, review and reflect. Then they complete the second narrative worksheet. Briefly they discuss or ask for clarifications.

Step Four: Then the large group is involved in debriefing. The Mediator leads by asking the general questions. In future lessons, students begin to take this role.

Step Five: After achieving proficiency in asking General Questions and mediating the students' responses, students learn how to pose more specific mediated questions as well as broad and narrow questions.

Step Six: A discussion concerning their transcendent values or wisdom principles follows.

Shantistan Mediated Learning Probes

R. Feuerstein (1980), adapted by Ruth V. Burgess, © (2005)

1. **(intent)** In what manner did I exhibit that I had something significant to share?

2. **(reciprocity)** When did you decide both of us were learning together?

3. **(search for meaning) [-s]** In what ways do multiple perspectives help us in our search for meaning [s]?

4. **(transcendence)** How do transcendent values or wisdom principles assist in developing representational thought?

5. **(mental competence)** Why is a willingness or an orientation to learn necessary for positive problem solving?

6. **(self-regulation, including metacognition, metapraxis and control of mental behavior)** Explain what happens when you reflect and regulate on your thinking.

7. **(individuation and group identity)** Give examples when individual and group identities may cause positive or negative disequilibrium.

8. **(belonging)** In what ways does the feeling of belonging assist in learning?

9. **(optimistic alternatives)** Explain the significance of maintaining an optimistic alternative.

10. **(self as a changing entity)** Propose how and why it is helpful to balance continuity and change.

(goals) Propose how setting goals, achieving goals and celebrating goals assists in developing proactive rather than reactive living skills.

(sharing) In how many ways can sharing become a peacemaking tool?

Shantistan Narrative: **INTEGRITY**

My Father, a Righteous Man
Patricia Nicholas, © 2008

Integrity is the first peace building theme. Family stories from our youth may help mold our future. Dr. Patricia A. Nicholas remembers such a life lesson from her teen age years.

Back in the old days when I was a teenager the popular thing to do was to go to a drive-in eating place to finish off a date.

One night my boyfriend and I joined several others at such a place called Rustins. It was a nice keepsake serving as a reminder of a wonderful time with my friends. The waitress brought out our tray of food plus an ash tray with "Rustins" painted on it. So I took it home and put it on my dresser.

My dad came into my bedroom to tell me good night and saw the ash tray. He asked me how I got it and why I wanted it since I did not smoke. I explained that ever took ashtrays as reminders of the good times they had at a particular place.

Well, my dad said that I was to get up out of bed, dress, and go with him. Of course, I did. He drove me back to Rustins. When we arrived Dad handed me the ash tray. I was to take it in and tell the manager that I had taken it and was now returning it as it was not mine.

The lesson was well learned and to this day never forgotten.

After Thoughts

Describe the two contexts in the story.

Explaining the significance of "integrity" in enabling a land of peace.

What are the cultural differences in this story from your youth?

Prepare a graphic that illustrates this Shantistan narrative theme.

Write its title in your birth language.

Shantistan Narrative: **HARMONY**

Mud in Your Eye
Robby Kagarise. © 2019

On one of my brother Rowdy's mission trips to Indonesia was to assist an area hardest hit by a tsunami. Among his experiences was the seemingly mundane task of helping to rebuild a community bathroom facility.

Work on the facility included pinning together with metal brackets and bolts to concrete barriers that had been broken loose from their moorings by the tsunami wave. Rowdy worked to drill holes through the concrete where bolts would run and then mount the brackets. Unfortunately the largest drill bit available was not quite adequate for the task. So after drilling through the wall Rowdy had to work the bit back and forth and around the hold to enlarge it.

The difficult process was complicated by the dust and debris that filled the holes. Another team member took up position of the other side of the wall, and occasionally Rowdy would stoop drilling and call for the other man to blow the dirt back through the hole. Before he resumed drilling, Rowdy would then peer through the hold to see if it looked large enough to accommodate a bolt.

Rowdy paused his drilling to peer into the wall. This time; however, the man on the other side did not wait for a verbal signal. He blew firmly into it just as Rowdy bent to peer in from the opposite side. Fortunately, sunglasses kept it from going directly in his eyes. He made a sound of surprise. In an instant he burst out in laughter. He pointed to his fact covered with red grime. Rowdy continued to work.

A bit later the interpreter spoke to him. "This is very good."

"What is?"

"All of the men could not understand why you didn't get into a fight. If that had happened to any of them they would have beat up the other man." Later that day this act of harmony spared another fellow after being soaked in a ditch.

After Thoughts

Distinguish the different perspectives in this story.

How is "harmony" a theme when enabling peace making?

Prepare a graphic that illustrates this *Shantistan* narrative theme.

Write its title in your birth language.

TOLERANCE

Bloods All Red

David Burgess, © age 11, 1985

Why did they leave me all alone?
Do they not know that they are my home?
I have no place to lay my head
I have no one to weep if I'm dead.
White or black, yellow or brown
Don't they know the bloods all red?
From prince to pauper, from cloak to crown
Don't they know the bloods all red?

Social Darwinism, Rise to the top
You gotta know where to stop
Evolution and the caste system
Since God made us all like him.

I don't know you're not from these parts
Don't you - I can tell you apart?
You got different skin, you're not one of us.'
You won't get hurt if you don't put up a fuss.

After Thoughts

What voices can be heard in this poem?

How can tolerance be a positive virtue in contemporary society?

Prepare a graphic that illustrates this *Shantistan* narrative theme.

Write its title in your birth language.

Shantistan Narrative **DEVOTION TO BELIEFS**

Where Has It Gone?
David Burgess, © age 11, 1985

Is the liberty and justice here in the U.S.A.?
Or has it gone out with Ms. Liberty's copper plate body?

Or the things we fought and shed our blood for slipping away?
Like Ms. Liberty's corroded torch?

Are the words, "Give us your tired, weak and huddled masses,
Being lost in all the madness?

Let me ask you one more thing,
Where Has It Gone?

After Thoughts

Justify how devotion to heritage beliefs impact one's life and death practices.

Write a transcendent value relating to one's spirit and mind. (Transcendent values are beliefs that extend beyond person, place, thing, and circumstance.)

Prepare a graphic that illustrates this *Shantistan* narrative theme.

Write its title in your birth language.

Tough Love

Ruth V. Burgess. © 2020

Matt, Scott, Mandy, and Davey accompanied their parents to Tantur, Israel in 1986. Tantur looked like a white stone medieval fortress on the top of a Judean hill. This ecumenical compound is located between Jerusalem and Bethlehem and down the road from Gilo. The daily morning Israeli helicopter buzzes, the hushed nightly Arabic conversations under bedroom windows, and bilingual accounts of disputed land provided negative disequilibrium for the quartet.

It was after celebrating the three different Christmas times that some unusual things were discovered. First, the children built a U.S.A. fort high on the pine needles, while the Yugoslavian children build a fort lower down the hill in a gulley. Davey discovered Byzantine tile and began cleaning them in the apartment bateau. His curiosity led him further to the stone entrance gate. Encased in a room on the right side was an ancient tomb of some man – possibly a crusader? Then he heard some whimpers from the upper chambers. It sounded like a frightened animal.

Going to the other side, Davey climbed the steps and saw the locked iron gate. Inside was a brown puppy with large dark eyes. "Oh, come here puppy. I won't hurt you," said Davey. "Better yet, my brothers and I will bring you some food."

Each day the brothers took turns slipping food to their new found friend. Slowly the puppy gained trust in them. Then he began to accept food from their hands.

Then on a balmy spring evening, dark shadows began outlining the Judean hills and the western sky turned from blue to royal purple hues. A faint sea breeze slowly rafted up the olive and apricot groves spreading the oncoming night scene. Two Arab men, one the night watchman and the other was his cousin-brother, settled back on their haunches on the rock wall and lit thin cigarettes. Soon giggles and anticipatory comments were heard wafting up the stone steps. The three brothers emerged with part of their supper tucked in flat bread. Quickly they ran up the tower steps. Eager to see Puppy, they began calling his name. There was no response. Again they called "Puppy" as they pressed their faces against the iron bars of the tower gate. Puppy was gone. The space was empty.

Scott and David ran down the stone steps to the two Arab men. "Where is Puppy? Where is he? We have food for him. Please, where have you put him?"

"He is dead. When one learns to love, one cannot kill," replied the Arab.

After Thoughts

Contrast the two approaches experienced at the ecumenical center.

Propose a path toward reconciliation of actions.

Prepare a graphic that illustrates the **Shantistan** Narrative theme. Write its title in your birth language.

Mother Teresa
Mother Teresa Center. © 2020

"I had the most extraordinary experience of love of a neighbor with a Hindu family. A gentleman came to our house and said, 'Mother Teresa, there is a family who has not eaten for so long. Do something.'

So I took some rice and went there immediately. And I saw the children - their eyes shining with hunger. I don't know if you have ever seen hunger. But I have seen it very often. And the mother of the family took the rice I gave her and she went out.

When she came back, I asked her, "Where did you go? What did you do?" And she gave me a very simple answer, 'They are hungry also.'

What struck me was that she knew - and who are they?

A Muslim family - and she knew. I didn't bring any more rice that evening because I wanted them, Hindus and Muslims, to enjoy the joy of sharing.

But there were those children, radiating joy and peace with their mother because she had the love to give until it hurts. And you see this is where love begins – at home in the family."

After Thoughts

Identify central issues in this life experience story

Formulate appropriate questions of the persons in this narrative

Predict probable consequences.

Transcendent Principle: *"True love which costs us something can transcend all boundaries."*

Marla of Chicago
Ruth V. Burgess. © 2019

Landing at Lode Airport in Tel Aviv and the subsequent cheroot ride up the mountains into Jerusalem had thrown Marla into a pensive mood. She was once again a pre-teen gathering apricots on her grandfather's farm in Greece. The strong smells of virgin olive oil and crusty wheat bread wafted from nearby windows.

She recalled the deep bass chants of the Greek Orthodox priest from the domed church on the far side of the aqua ducts. His mother's words. Grandmother's words. What was it they said? "Every day do something to help someone." A smile floated over Marla's face. This journey was to be a special time; she wanted to recapture the innocence, now absent in the Chicago rat race.

The cooing of the doves mingled with the jarring clatter of the Israeli helicopter announced her first day in the hold land. After drinking hot Arab coffee with crusty bread spread with goats butter and fig jam, Marla walked down the remains of the Rome rock road. Slowing her pace on the uneven rocks, Marla reached the paved road leading down the mountain towards Bethlehem. Surely, there was someone she could help in that blessed city today.

Slowly approaching from the distant valley was a man with something on his head. Ah, it appears to be a blind many with a donkey. Both were burdened down with long firewood sticks. Greeting him in Arabic and English, Marla explained that according to her religious beliefs she should help someone every day. God had sent him to her. On both the first and second day the blind man rebuffed Marla's help. He used a loud voice and waved one arm towards her.

By the dawning of the third day, Marla's said her early morning prayers in the ecumenical chapel. Going down the same paths, Marla noticed something different. There was the donkey, the blind man, and a younger man. "Oh, good," spoke Marla to the Judean wind, "Maybe the young man can speak English." Quickening her steps, soon they meet. Before Marla could speak, the young man said, "My uncle requested that I accompany him today, because there had been a crazy woman accosting him for the past two days. My uncle says he would rather be blind than to be followed by a crazy woman. Please leave us alone."

After Thoughts

Hypothesize the multiple levels of meaning within the story.

What background experiences did you bring to this multicultural story?

Prepare a graphic that illustrates the *Shantistan* Narrative theme. Write its title in your birth language.

Pomp and Ceremony
Ruth V. Burgess. © 2019

The Bentley was polished and shinning. The leather shown with red umber salve. Proper .dress, laced shoes and sun helmets were selected. Sandal wood soap was purchased with prized rupees. The driver was dressed to the hilt and was honored to be driving to the ancient palace. Upon arriving the young couple, Gladys and Maynard, were enthralled with the brilliant landscape. The grounds were impeccable manicured, brilliant flowers adorned pedestals and honor guards, with their brass adornments shining as gold, stood at attention. Guests posed according to rank and courtesy expectations.

In about three hours the royal entourage arrived. The welcome ceremony began with bows, courtesies, nods and polite salutations. Gladys was not enjoying this ceremonial occasion. She kept whispering to Maynard that they needed to slip out and go back to the mission compound. She was tired and wanted to go home. Surely, no one would notice their absence.

Finally, Maynard succumbed to his newly wed wife's pleas. They slipped toward the royal garage and asked for their Bentley. The keeper said that he could not comply. Showing the spirit of the "west," Maynard and Gladys walked to their car and started down the roadway. Outside of the gates and all the way to the next village there were people lining the sides of the road. They were bowing, saluting, chanting, singing, waving flags and paying homage. Not knowing what to do, Maynard waved to them.

On the following day Maynard received a white chite (note) asking why the Ketchums left early. When the British Consulate General left there were no people left on the sides of the road to pay homage to him.

After Thoughts

How is "human dignity" defined in your culture?

In what manner should peacemakers respect "human dignity"?

Prepare a "quilt block" that illustrates "human dignity". Write its title in your birth language.

The Man on the Street
Robbie Kagarise. © 2020

One day as my two brothers, adolescents at the time, were out with my dad going to some stores, we saw a man in the street at a nearby intersection. The man was wandering around acting erratically. He looked haggard and dirty. It became clear that he was drunk. As he stumbled around, falling and getting up, people shouted angrily at him or made fun of him from their car windows. His replies only made a bigger fool of himself.

As my brothers looked on with youthful fascination at something they had never seen before, my dad suddenly told them to stay where they were. Dad walked away from them, crossing part of a parking lot. To their surprise, he walked right toward the drunken man. With people still shouting and laughing at the man, dad walked out into the street to his side. He helped him regain his balance and led him by the arm off of the thoroughfare. With the man away from the street, the sideshow atmosphere quickly disappeared as new traffic rolled through. We watched as dad helped the man sit down and talked with him shortly.

Dad returned to where my brothers were, never saying much of anything about what had happened. But dad had just taught us something about the way human beings should regard one another.

After Thoughts

Who benefitted from the virtue shown by the father?

Explain the significance of a culture bearer across generations.

Prepare a graphic that illustrates this *Shantistan* narrative theme. Write its title in your birth language.

The Favorite Son
Ruth Burgess. © 2020

Few stories are recorded in five different religions over three millennia. Even as geo-political boundaries changed, the Joseph story continued to be passed forward. We find it in the Hebrew Midrash, Christian Old and New Testaments, Islam (Sunni Koran), Babi religion, Baha faith, Egyptian literature, and Zoroaster texts. Some of The following themes intrigue one's imagination.

1. Jacob, the father, had a favorite son by his beloved wife Rachel. Joseph was handsome, a dreamer and intelligent.

2. Joseph brothers were jealous and conspired to murder him, but opted selling him to desert traders. Later he is charged with seducing Potipher's wife (Zulaikha), who was an idol worshipper. Earlier she had fallen in love with Joseph in a dream, but he was true to his God and remained morally pure.

3. Due to positive economic and management policies, Egypt under Joseph's guidance was able to avoid famine and even provided grain to Jacob's family, including his former devious brothers.

4. Joseph forgives his brothers and is reunited with his family in Egypt.

5. In one rendition, Zulaikha, now a blind, old woman in the marketplace, disposes her idols and goes to the palace and pleads her everlasting love for Joseph, who now is Egypt's Grand Vizier.

This parable has different levels of meaning. It is a spiritual journey played out in voices heard from heaven as well as here on earth.

After Thoughts

Contemplate the different types of forgiveness Joseph showed in his lifetime.

Share a parable or wisdom saying that supports the use of "faith practice."

PROTECTION OF LIFE
How do we reconcile compassion in hopes of maintaining peace?

Ahmedabad is Burning
Ruth Burgess © 2020

One block from my sister's house was a war zone! Buses, scooters, buildings burning. Stones were in the road to block the way. Tensions filled the smoky sky. This was war against our ... yours and mine ... Indian brothers and sisters. We who live on this planet belong to each other.

Later they went to a Hindu area where they passed out food packets and soap to women. There were some widows. These belong to the Jain set. They are good non-violent people. They do not eat anything from the ground, such as onion, garlic, or potatoes. They do not want to risk eating an insect. Earlier twenty of their group was burned alive in the Muslim train bogey atrocity. They showed us their temple. This was their hope for safety.

Compassion knows no community. Compassion knows not caste. Compassion draws no lines as we are taught to understand. Psalm 11 says God hates men who do violent acts. WOW! Our survival on this planet is vital to peaceful co-existence.

Lord, help! Hindus did puja in the Muslim mosque, thus defiling the Muslim's holy place. Can you picture the anti-Christ sitting in the temple? Whose temple? People are going to believe he is the real thing. Why? Is it possible that in our lifetime this dispensation will come to an end?

After Thoughts
Reflect on the following comments:

* *Unconditional love was both a solstice and a caretaker of peace.*
* *Unlimited love required love to suffer with the hurting and dying.*
* *Love required that care must be shown at every level, to both the innocent and guilty.*

* *Love did not flow like a raging river out of its banks, but came like delicate raindrops soaking through the heads into the hearts of the suffering.*
* *When war comes everyone is crushed.*

The title of my story _____

SACRIFICE

Sacrifice may be considered a virtue.

All for a Son

Ruth Burgess. © 2020

For over two hundred years the Takker tribe maintained their vow not to work for a white man. Colonial Brits had been proven untrustworthy. Now Vassar Sahib asked them to dynamite granite from the quarry to build a two story dormitory for the orphan boys living in Junnar Orphanage. It was disconcerting when the reconnaissance team reported that the new superintendent served a god that loved children. If this be so, then the Takker's would give the job a trial run.

Three years later a friendly delegation walked down the Deccan mountainous path to meet with Vassar Sahib on the mission compound. Bap Rao led three women, two young girls and a baby cuddled in a red and white rice cloth. This company shared the usual greetings about the weather, crops and the encroaching government policies. Then Mr. Rao explained that he wanted to talk about his god.

It seems that after their lugna (wedding ceremony) he and his wife went to the temple and did puja. They asked for a son. She became pregnant and he felt god was preparing a son for their home. Alas, the baby was a girl. Guilt filled his being. How could this be? The old village widow said that the family had not done enough puja, or else they would have been blessed with a son.

Perhaps the old woman was right. The men planned a pilgrimage to the holy river beyond the rocky mountains. They took alms, and bathed as they prayed for a son. Wonderful! My wife became pregnant again. Praise god. A son is on the way. But alas, it was another daughter. Am I damned?

I listened to the elders' advice in the family evening circle. It was the common belief that my wife had the devil in her. So I defaced her. I had to get evil out of her.

Sir, look at my wife now. She is holding our beloved son.

After Thoughts

Discuss Sacrifice as it applies to the different persons in the story.

Why are "old school" and "new school" ideas or practices be difficult to differentiate or accept?

Prepare a "quilt" block that illustrates this narrative theme. Write its title in your birth language.

The title of my narrative _____

74

The Peacemaker
Fifteenth Century India Legend

The Maharajah's mighty army marched forward as the brass horns blared of trouble that was to come. The parched earth shook as the massive columns of elephants tramped. Corpses were left rotting in the fields and huts burned. Mothers cried for sons to return and waited for husbands, who were not seen. This egocentric war dragged on. Only one person was committed to ending the mayhem.

Princess Tulsi, the beautiful Maharaja's daughter, was determined that the fighting must end. Colleagues tried to discourage her by saying, "You are only a girl, or "You are too young to make a difference." Not heeding their remarks, Tulsi swept past the guards protecting the council chamber. "I want to see the Maharajah."

The Maharajah was surprised. "Go to your quarters, daughter. War is a business for men, not girls."

"My dear father, I do not speak of war. I want to talk of peace. Why don't you go over to the king that you are fighting. Ask him what he meant by his initial letter? Let's go talk with him."

At the neighboring province, the king spoke first, "What did you mean, Maharajah, by your message - "Send fifty blue pigs or else..."?

"Fifty blue pigs," explained the Maharajah, "or else white pigs or black pigs or any other color that is available. What did you mean...?

"Oh," replied the king, "if you had carried on reading you would have seen. My message was, "We have got no blue pigs for you and if we had I would be most pleased to send them to you."

At once the kings comprehended their misunderstanding. The war was stopped, the soldiers came home, and the country returned to peace and plenty. But of all the treasures the Maharajah loved best was his daughter, Tulsi the peacemaker.

After Thoughts

State a rule or wisdom principles whereby Tulsi learned about peacemaking.

Identify and then rank several principles of reconciliation found in contemporary society.

Prepare a graphic that illustrates the *Shantistan* Narrative theme. Write its title in your birth language.

Shantistan Narrative Chart

dates s: started c: completed	*Shantistan* **themes**	Title of narrative or sayings	Name of source /-s	Transcendent principle or values
s: c:	1. Integrity			
s: c:	2. Harmony			
s: c:	3. Tolerance			
s: c:	4. Devotion to Beliefs			
s: c:	5. Love			
s: c:	6. Doing Good			
s: c:	7. Civility			
s: c:	8. Human Dignity			
s: c:	9. Human Kindness			
s: c:	10. Faith & Forgiveness			
s: c:	11. Protection of Life			
s: c:	12. Sacrifice			
s: c:	13. Reconciliation			

Supplement C

Narrative Forms

1. Integrity, form
2. Harmony, form
3. Tolerance, form
4. Devotion to Belief, form
5. Love, form
6. Doing Good, form
7. Civility, form
8. Human Dignity, form
9. Human Kind, form
10. Faith and Forgiveness, form
11. Protection of Life, form
12. Sacrifice, form
13. Reconciliation, form

©*Shantistan* **Theme Quilt**.
Made by Elizabeth Dotson, 2019

Note the multicolor hands that are labeled "Reconciliation" encircle the other twelve *Shantistan* concepts.

LIFE NARRATIVES   Ruth Burgess © 2005

INTEGRITY

A. DEFINITION
   Integrity is

B. HERITAGE NARRATIVE EXAMPLE: Title _____
   If the story is short, please write the narrative below. If it is longer,
   write a shortened version or write an annotated bibliographic citation.

C. IN WHAT WAYS DOES THIS LIFE NARRATIVE ILLUSTRATE
   INTEGRITY?

D. EXPLAIN WHY **INTEGRITY** IS RELEVANT WHEN ONE IS
   PEACEBUILDING.

Name _____ Date _____

Shantistan

Ruth Burgess © 2005

INTEGRITY

1. Read your associates paper relating to **integrity.**

2. ETHNOLOGIC REFLECTIONS

   From past experiences, identify the ways your associate's understandings are alike or different from yours. Make a check mark in the column that describes your belief.

	Same	similar	different	other
Definition				
Heritage narrative example				
Application of **integrity** concept to Peacebuilding.				

3. QUESTIONS I WOULD LIKE TO ASK OF MY ASSOCIATE:

   a.

   b.

   c.

4. WRITE A TRANSCENDENT VALUE OR PRINCIPLE THAT CAN BE EXTRACTED FROM THIS LESSON.

Name _____ Date _____

LIFE NARRATIVES   Ruth Burgess © 2005

HARMONY

A. DEFINITION
   Harmony is

B. HERITAGE NARRATIVE EXAMPLE: Title _____
   If the story is short, please write the narrative below. If it is longer,
   write a shortened version or write an annotated bibliographic citation.

C. IN WHAT WAYS DOES THIS LIFE NARRATIVE ILLUSTRATE
   HARMONY?

D. EXPLAIN WHY **HARMONY** IS RELEVANT WHEN ONE IS
   PEACEBUILDING.

Name _____ Date _____

LIFE NARRATIVES   Ruth Burgess © 2005

HARMONY

1. Read your associates paper relating to **harmony.**
2. ETHNOLOGIC REFLECTIONS

    From past experiences, identify the ways your associate's understandings are alike or different from yours. Make a check mark in the column that describes your belief.

	Same	similar	different	other
Definition				
Heritage narrative example				
Application of **harmony** concept to Peacebuilding.				

3. QUESTIONS I WOULD LIKE TO ASK OF MY ASSOCIATE:

    a.

    b.

    c.

4. WRITE A TRANSCENDENT VALUE OR WISDOM PRINCIPLE THAT CAN BE EXTRACTED FROM THIS LESSON.

Name _____ Date _____

LIFE NARRATIVES   Ruth Burgess © 2005

TOLERANCE

A. DEFINITION
   Tolerance is

   Multiple Perspectives evolve as

B. HERITAGE NARRATIVE EXAMPLE: Title _____
   If the story is short, please write the narrative below. If it is longer,
   write a shortened version or write an annotated bibliographic citation.

C. IN WHAT WAYS DOES THIS LIFE NARRATIVE ILLUSTRATE
   Tolerance Toward Multiple Perspectives?

D. EXPLAIN WHY **Tolerance** IS RELEVANT WHEN ONE IS
   PEACEBUILDING.

Name _____ Date _____

LIFE NARRATIVES   Ruth Burgess © 2005

TOLERANCE

1. Read your associates paper relating to **tolerance and flexibility towards multiple perspectives.**

2. ETHNOLOGIC REFLECTIONS

   From past experiences, identify the ways your associate's understandings are alike or different from yours. Make a check mark in the column that describes your belief.

	Same	similar	different	other
Definition				
Heritage narrative example				
Application of **tolerance** concept to Peacebuilding.				

3. QUESTIONS I WOULD LIKE TO ASK OF MY ASSOCIATE:

   a.

   b.

   c.

4. WRITE A TRANSCENDENT VALUE OR PRINCIPLE THAT CAN BE EXTRACTED FROM THIS LESSON.

Name _____ Date _____

LIFE NARRATIVES

DEVOTION TO BELIEFS

A. **DEFINITION**

Devotion to one's beliefs is

Self or group honor evolves as

B. **HERITAGE NARRATIVE EXAMPLE:** Title _____

If the story is short, please write the narrative below. If it is longer, write a shortened version or write an annotated bibliographic citation.

C. IN WHAT WAYS DOES THIS LIFE NARRATIVE ILLUSTRATE **devotion to one's beliefs or group honor?**

D. EXPLAIN WHY **SELF AND GROUP HONOR** ARE RELEVANT WHEN ONE IS PEACEBUILDING.

Name _____ Date _____

LIFE NARRATIVES   Ruth Burgess © 2005

DEVOTION TO BELIEFS

1. Read your associate's paper relating to **Devotion To Beliefs.**
2. ETHNOLOGIC REFLECTIONS

   From past experiences, identify the ways your associate's understandings are alike or different from yours. Make a check mark in the column that describes your belief.

	Same	similar	different	other
Definition				
Heritage narrative example				
Application of **devotion to belief** concept to Peacebuilding.				

3. QUESTIONS I WOULD LIKE TO ASK OF MY ASSOCIATE:

   a.

   b.

   c.

4. WRITE A TRANSCENDENT VALUE OR PRINCIPLE THAT CAN BE EXTRACTED FROM THIS LESSON.

Name _____ Date _____

LIFE NARRATIVES   Ruth Burgess © 2005

LOVE

A. DEFINITION (Are there different types of love?)
   Love is

B. HERITAGE NARRATIVE EXAMPLE: Title _____
   If the story is short, please write the narrative below. If it is longer,
   write a shortened version or write an annotated bibliographic citation.

C. IN WHAT WAYS DOES THIS LIFE NARRATIVE ILLUSTRATE
   LOVE?

D. EXPLAIN WHY **LOVE** IS RELEVANT WHEN ONE IS
   PEACEBUILDING.

Name _____ Date _____

LIFE NARRATIVES   Ruth Burgess © 2005

LOVE

1. Read your associate's paper relating to **LOVE.**

2. ETHNOLOGIC REFLECTIONS

   From past experiences, identify the ways your associate's understandings are alike or different from yours. Make a check mark in the column that describes your belief.

	Same	similar	different	other
Definition				
Heritage narrative example				
Application of **love** concept to Peacebuilding.				

3. QUESTIONS I WOULD LIKE TO ASK OF MY ASSOCIATE:

   a.

   b.

   c.

4. WRITE A TRANSCENDENT VALUE OR PRINCIPLE THAT CAN BE EXTRACTED FROM THIS LESSON.

Name _____ Date _____

LIFE NARRATIVES   Ruth Burgess © 2005

DOING GOOD

A. DEFINITION
   Doing Good means

   Are **Doing Good** and **Charity** the same thing?

B. HERITAGE NARRATIVE EXAMPLE: Title _____
   If the story is short, please write the narrative below. If it is longer,
   write a shortened version or write an annotated bibliographic citation.

C. IN WHAT WAYS DOES THIS LIFE NARRATIVE ILLUSTRATE
   Doing Good?

D. EXPLAIN WHY **Doing Good** IS RELEVANT WHEN ONE IS
   PEACEBUILDING.

Name _____ Date _____

LIFE NARRATIVES   Ruth Burgess © 2005

DOING GOOD

1. Read your associate's paper relating to **Doing Good.**
2. ETHNOLOGIC REFLECTIONS

    From past experiences, identify the ways your associate's understandings are alike or different from yours. Make a check mark in the column that describes your belief.

	Same	similar	different	other
Definition				
Heritage narrative example				
Application of **doing good** concept to Peacebuilding.				

3. QUESTIONS I WOULD LIKE TO ASK OF MY ASSOCIATE:

    a.

    b.

    c.

4. WRITE A TRANSCENDENT VALUE OR PRINCIPLE THAT CAN BE EXTRACTED FROM THIS LESSON.

Name _____ Date _____

LIFE NARRATIVES Ruth Burgess © 2005

CIVILITY

A. DEFINITION
   CIVILITY means

   In what ways can **civility** be shown or recognized?

B. HERITAGE NARRATIVE EXAMPLE: Title _____
   If the story is short, please write the narrative below. If it is longer,
   write a shortened version or write an annotated bibliographic citation.

C. IN WHAT WAYS DOES THIS LIFE NARRATIVE ILLUSTRATE
   CIVILITY?

D. EXPLAIN WHY **CIVILITY** IS RELEVANT WHEN ONE IS
   PEACEBUILDING.

Name _____ Date _____

LIFE NARRATIVES   Ruth Burgess © 2005

CIVILITY

1. Read your associate's paper relating to **Doing Civility.**

2. ETHNOLOGIC REFLECTIONS

    From past experiences, identify the ways your associate's understandings are alike or different from yours. Make a check mark in the column that describes your belief.

	Same	similar	different	other
Definition				
Heritage narrative example				
Application of **doing civil** concept to Peacebuilding.				

3. QUESTIONS I WOULD LIKE TO ASK OF MY ASSOCIATE:

    a.

    b.

    c.

4. Write a transcendent value or wisdom principle that can be extracted from this lesson.

Name _____ Date _____

LIFE NARRATIVES   Ruth Burgess © 2005

HUMAN DIGNITY

A. DEFINITION
   Human Dignity means

B. HERITAGE NARRATIVE EXAMPLE: Title _____
   If the story is short, please write the narrative below. If it is longer, write a shortened version or write an annotated bibliographic citation.

C. IN WHAT WAYS DOES THIS LIFE NARRATIVE ILLUSTRATE **HUMAN DIGNITY?**

D. EXPLAIN WHY **HUMAN DIGNITY** IS RELEVANT WHEN ONE IS PEACEBUILDING.

Name _____ Date _____

Shantistan

Ruth Burgess © 2005

HUMAN DIGNITY

1. Read your associate's paper relating to **Human Dignity.**
2. ETHNOLOGIC REFLECTIONS

   From past experiences, identify the ways your associate's understandings are alike or different from yours. Make a check mark in the column that describes your belief.

	Same	similar	different	other
Definition				
Heritage narrative example				
Application of **human dignity** concept to Peacebuilding.				

3. QUESTIONS I WOULD LIKE TO ASK OF MY ASSOCIATE:

   a.

   b.

   c.

4. WRITE A TRANSCENDENT VALUE OR PRINCIPLE THAT CAN BE EXTRACTED FROM THIS LESSON.

Name _____ Date _____

LIFE NARRATIVES   Ruth Burgess © 2005

BROTHERHOOD/SISTERHOOD

A. DEFINITION
    Brotherhood means

    Sisterhood means

    Personhood means

B. HERITAGE NARRATIVE EXAMPLE: Title _____
    If the story is short, please write the narrative below. If it is longer,
    write a shortened version or write an annotated bibliographic citation.

C. IN WHAT WAYS DOES THIS LIFE NARRATIVE ILLUSTRATE
    BROTHERHOOD?

D. EXPLAIN WHY **BROTHERHOOD** IS RELEVANT WHEN
    ONE IS PEACEBUILDING.

Name _____ Date _____

BROTHERHOOD/SISTERHOOD

1. Read your associate's paper relating to **Brotherhood/Sisterhood.**
2. ETHNOLOGIC REFLECTIONS

   From past experiences, identify the ways your associate's understandings are alike or different from yours. Make a check mark in the column that describes your belief.

	Same	similar	different	other
Definition				
Heritage narrative example				
Application of **brotherhood** concept to Peacebuilding.				

3. QUESTIONS I WOULD LIKE TO ASK OF MY ASSOCIATE:

   a.

   b.

   c.

4. WRITE A TRANSCENDENT VALUE OR PRINCIPLE THAT CAN BE EXTRACTED FROM THIS LESSON.

Name _____ Date _____

LIFE NARRATIVES   Ruth Burgess © 2005

FAITH AND FORGIVENESS

A. DEFINITION

   Faith means

   Forgiveness means

B. HERITAGE NARRATIVE EXAMPLE: Title _____

   If the story is short, please write the narrative below. If it is longer, write a shortened version or write an annotated bibliographic citation.

C. IN WHAT WAYS DOES THIS LIFE NARRATIVE ILLUSTRATE **Faith and Forgiveness?**

D. EXPLAIN WHY **Faith and Forgiveness** IS RELEVANT WHEN ONE IS PEACEBUILDING.

Name _____ Date _____

Shantistan

Ruth Burgess © 2005

FAITH AND FORGIVENESS

1. Read your associate's paper relating to **Faith and Forgiveness.**
2. ETHNOLOGIC REFLECTIONS

    From past experiences, identify the ways your associate's understandings are alike or different from yours. Make a check mark in the column that describes your belief.

	Same	similar	different	other
Definition				
Heritage narrative example				
Application of **Faith and Forgiveness** concept to Peacebuilding.				

3. QUESTIONS I WOULD LIKE TO ASK OF MY ASSOCIATE:

    a.

    b.

    c.

4. WRITE A TRANSCENDENT VALUE OR PRINCIPLE THAT CAN BE EXTRACTED FROM THIS LESSON.

Name _____ Date _____

LIFE NARRATIVES Ruth Burgess © 2005

PROTECTION OF LIFE

A. DEFINITION
   PROTECTION OF LIFE means

B. HERITAGE NARRATIVE EXAMPLE: Title _____
   If the story is short, please write the narrative below. If it is longer, write a shortened version or write an annotated bibliographic citation.

C. IN WHAT WAYS DOES THIS LIFE NARRATIVE ILLUSTRATE **Protection Of Life?**

D. EXPLAIN WHY **Protection Of Life** IS RELEVANT WHEN ONE IS PEACEBUILDING.

Name _____ Date _____

LIFE NARRATIVES 5.3 (11.2)   Ruth Burgess © 2005

PROTECTION OF LIFE

1. Read your associate's paper relating to **Protection Of Life.**

2. ETHNOLOGIC REFLECTIONS

    From past experiences, identify the ways your associate's understandings are alike or different from yours. Make a check mark in the column that describes your belief.

	Same	similar	different	other
Definition				
Heritage narrative example				
Application of **Protection of Life** concept to Peacebuilding.				

3. QUESTIONS I WOULD LIKE TO ASK OF MY ASSOCIATE:

    a.

    b.

    c.

4. WRITE A TRANSCENDENT VALUE OR PRINCIPLE THAT CAN BE EXTRACTED FROM THIS LESSON.

Name _____ Date _____

SACRIFICE

A. DEFINITION
    Sacrifice means

B. HERITAGE NARRATIVE EXAMPLE: Title _____
    If the story is short, please write the narrative below. If it is longer,
    write a shortened version or write an annotated bibliographic citation.

C. IN WHAT WAYS DOES THIS LIFE NARRATIVE ILLUSTRATE
    Sacrifice?

D. EXPLAIN WHY **Sacrifice** IS RELEVANT WHEN ONE IS
    PEACEBUILDING.

Name _____ Date _____

LIFE NARRATIVES   Ruth Burgess © 2005

SACRIFICE

1. Read your associate's paper relating to **Sacrifice.**

2. ETHNOLOGIC REFLECTIONS

   From past experiences, identify the ways your associate's understandings are alike or different from yours. Make a check mark in the column that describes your belief.

	Same	similar	different	other
Definition				
Heritage narrative example				
Application of **Sacrifice** concept to Peacebuilding.				

3. QUESTIONS I WOULD LIKE TO ASK OF MY ASSOCIATE:

   a.

   b.

   c.

4. WRITE A TRANSCENDENT VALUE OR PRINCIPLE THAT CAN BE EXTRACTED FROM THIS LESSON.

Name _____ Date _____

LIFE NARRATIVES   Ruth Burgess © 2005

RECONCILIATION

A. DEFINITION
   Reconciliation means

B. HERITAGE NARRATIVE EXAMPLE: Title _____
   If the story is short, please write the narrative below. If it is longer,
   write a shortened version or write an annotated bibliographic citation.

C. IN WHAT WAYS DOES THIS LIFE NARRATIVE ILLUSTRATE
   Reconciliation?

D. EXPLAIN WHY **Reconcilition** IS RELEVANT WHEN ONE IS
   PEACEBUILDING.

Name _____ Date _____

LIFE NARRATIVES   Ruth Burgess © 2005

RECONCILIATION

1. Read your associate's paper relating to **Reconciliation.**

2. ETHNOLOGIC REFLECTIONS

    From past experiences, identify the ways your associate's understandings are alike or different from yours. Make a check mark in the column that describes your belief.

	Same	similar	different	other
Definition				
Heritage narrative example				
Application of **Reconciliation** concept to Peacebuilding.				

3. QUESTIONS I WOULD LIKE TO ASK OF MY ASSOCIATE:

    a.

    b.

    c.

4. WRITE A TRANSCENDENT VALUE OR PRINCIPLE THAT CAN BE EXTRACTED FROM THIS LESSON.

Name _____ Date _____

SECTION THREE

Heritage Experiences

Heritage Box Exercise
Ruth Burgess. © 1999

INTRODUCTION

Several years ago I taught a course pertaining to Working with Families who had Individuals with Disabilities. For many of my students, coming to the university was their first separation from their families. Yes, this experience was yet another state certification course. The students appeared to be there to read, attend, take tests and adhere to the expected behavioral requirements.

But there was something missing. Somehow authentic relationships seemed lacking or missing among my students. As the teacher – mediator, how could I enable compassionate relationships among class members? Returning to learning theory, I recalled that Reuven Feuerstein (1980) wrote that cognition works on three types of mental content: heritage, contemporary experiences and scientific learning. Therefore, my initiative began with "How can I integrate my students' heritages into a meaning activity?" Additionally, "How can this experience incorporate the significance of insider perspectives versus outsider perspectives?"

From these imperatives the Heritage Box exercise was created. Heritage boxes or containers bring insight into private heritage collections that may have the opportunity to assess the resources and values available to forbearers. These artifacts illustrate the function performed both in public and private lives, as well as one's forbearers' appreciation for esthetics. Some families maintain and collect artifacts as a means of continuing family memory. The condition of the artifacts may reflect use or how they were preserved in the meantime.

Why is the study of heritage important? Heritage knowledge gives self and group identities. The intergenerational transmission of heritage promotes the continuance of how families make and seek meaning. This heritage logic, or ethnologic, provides a system that enables the young to develop representational thought. Furthermore, if a family values its heritage, then they should value those who can transmit this prized heritage into the future. Who might these people be? Our children.

"Everyone comes with their past.
This past is to be respected in that it has directly
affected the family now." Laurie

Heritage Boxes bring insights into private heritage collections that have been passed down intergenerationally. In these collections, we have the opportunity to assess the resources available to forebearers. The artifacts illustrate the functions performed both in public and private lives, as well as one's forebearers appreciation for esthetics. Some families maintain and collect artifacts as a means of continuing family memory. The condition of the artifacts may reflect use or how they were preserved in the meantime.

One must remember we are outside their time and space. We build our understanding of them based on our experiences, heritage transmission, and formal education. To further understand their context, we read the formal accounts in history and view the changes that were made to the land. Both the formal and informal accounts provide valuable clues so we may reconstruct a heritage complete with meaning. It is a heritage that contains both public and private meanings.

The private meanings become more real when we seek out the private stories, legends, humorous anecdotes, and other remembrances from family and trusted acquaintances. By gathering the formal and informal evidences we begin to see patterns emerging. These patterns may reflect our forebearers' beliefs and practices relating to economics, religion, political, family beliefs and practices, as well as attitudes toward change and continuity. In addition, the patterns may reflect their beliefs about preservation and conservation of the natural and constructed environments. Through scholarly endeavors we are better able to appreciate how one's forebearers fit into their larger context.

Why is the study of heritage important? Heritage knowledge gives self and group identities. The intergenerational transmission of heritage promotes the continuance of how families make and seek meaning. This heritage logic, or ethnologic, provides a system that enables the young to develop representational thought. Furthermore, if a family values its heritage, then they should value those who can transmit this prized heritage into the future. Who might these people be? Our children.

Sequence of the Heritage Box Project

Phase I: The Culture Bearer prepares for the project. (Heritage Box Introduction)

*   Teacher – Mediator gathers artifacts that will go into an example Heritage Box.
*   Prepares an introduction about preserving their heritage and finding artifacts.
*   Introduces the Heritage Box participant worksheets.
*   Prepares alternate project for those who experienced early traumas in their family. One suggestion is to select a book written for a juvenile readership and let the student create a heritage box for a fictional character.

Phase II: Finding Heritage Artifacts in nooks and crannies (My Heritage Box)

*   Share the value of locating one's heritage artifacts
*   Select a container to hold the artifacts. Most persons have stored their artifacts in boxes or baskets. One student brought a relative's body bag from the Vietnam War.

Phase III: Discovering Common and Uncommon Heritages (That Heritage Box, Heritage Box Inventory, Insider versus Outsider Opinions)

*   Students place their Heritage Boxes on a table, without commenting on the content.
*   They have the option of removing the top, or leaving the container covered.
*   The teacher systematically places a sticky note with an identifying number on each Heritage Box.
*   Then the students select a different box to record their impressions about this family.

* Often several students will select the same box. This means some Heritage Boxes will not be analyzed. This leads to asking, "What happens when the Heritage Boxes are not selected or analyzed?"

Phase IV: Presenting my Heritage Box to the cohort

* Depending on the class size, each person shares his Heritage Box with a small group.
* Since the students self-selected the contents there is usually a connection that if one does not preserve his heritage then there will be much forgotten or lost. For history usually records the deeds of the wealthy and famous.
* "I learned that although one may be able to look through the cultural artifacts and create an idea of the meanings of the items. It still takes further explanations by an insider, who truly understands his heritage. While the preserved artifacts may have significance to a family who keep them, it takes a storyteller to create a living narrative which is rich with meaning and significance."

Phase V: Insider Perspectives

* *"It is difficult to understand someone's heritage without talking to them or knowing about their past. It is easier to be biased when you have not had a chance to fully learn about it from them."* Carrie and Jenny.
* After the participants complete That Heritage Box experience, each student introduces his Heritage Box. Since the students self-selected the contents there is usually a connection that if one does not preserve his heritage then there will be much forgotten or lost. For history usually records the deeds and artifacts of the wealthy and famous.
* *"What we see on the outside is only part of the heritage the child brings with him."*
  Angela

My Heritage Box- example
Ruth Burgess. ©1999

by _____

date _____

Instructions: Write a brief narrative concerning your "Heritage Box." Here are some suggestions.

How was it you came across the artifacts?

What led to your decision to include them in the box?

What stories does this box hold? who preserved these artifacts? How and why have they been preserved?

What are your thoughts and feelings about your heritage?

What new information did you acquire through compilation of the heritage box?

Who will transmit your heritage into the future?

I have a wonderful aunt who is the mediator in our family. She has collected all these neat items throughout the years from my grandparents and great-grandparents. These people mean a lot to me. I was named after my grandfather "Albert."

The tin can is about my aunt's childhood drinking and eating cup. She used it at school during the depression. The notary paper is about my uncle's job in the Billing's bank. They lost everything in the depression.

The woman is my mother's sister. She gave me the picture of my mother. It is a rare picture as a young girl. I value my heritage because my relatives gave me a faith in God and values that give me strength in daily life. I discovered that my relatives left some diaries about life in the depression years. Hopefully I will be able to locate them.

I plan to be the next family mediator, so that a new generation will know the earlier generations.

If my heritage box had a name it would be <u>Two Cultures One Family</u>.

An inventory of my Heritage box is listed below:

Notary Stamper belonging to grandfather Albert. Aunt Barbara's tin cup. Brother's medical chart. Grandma Minne's pencil holder. Dad's name tag. Aunt Barbara's Bible. Man's picture. Grandpa's paper weight."

THAT HERITAGE BOX - example

Ruth Burgess. © 1999

Reporter

_____

_____

Place _____

Authorized by _____

Directions: select a "heritage box" to study and write a brief report (100 to 200 words). You are to describe the family who transmitted this heritage. Some questions are provided to guide your investigation.

1. In what time period did they live?
2. Describe the people who used these artifacts?
3. Where did these people live?
4. What impact did these people have on society (then and now)? What impact might these people have on the future? Support your conclusions.
5. Describe their family practices? What kind of problem solving approaches did they follow?
6. What evidence gives you information about their health, economic, political, religious, educational, or social status?
7. What impact on the land did these people make?
8. (other questions)

Persons lived in a recent time period. There is a picture of someone using a sewing machine. The people who used these had children (baby wipe container), possibly made clothing or sewed, possibly played cards. Maybe these people lived in a modern society, either urban or rural.

They may impact society by their parenting skills, sewing abilities. The future may also be affected by their parenting skills. If they were caring parents and may be a caring person, possibly a teacher as a profession. These people were healthy to bear children.

Economically they seem okay They were able to afford a sewing machine. Perhaps they made their own clothing. These people could be very family oriented. Maybe the woman was a stay at home mon.

The cards may be for casual fun - to preoccupy time or to use as gambling material. May have been used to keep something tried down or together – possible on a moving trip.

MY HERITAGE BOX

Ruth Burgess. © 1999

by _____

date _____

Instructions write a brief narrative concerning your "Heritage Box." How was it you came across the artifacts? What led to your decision to include them in the box? What stories does this box hold? who preserved these artifacts? How and why have they been preserved? What are your thoughts and feelings about your heritage? What new information did you acquire through compilation of the heritage box? Who will transmit your heritage into the future?

If my heritage box had a name it would be _____

An inventory of my heritage box is listed below:

THAT HERITAGE BOX

Ruth BURGESS. ©s 1999

Reporter _____

Date _____

Place _____

Authorized by _____

Directions: Select a "heritage box" to study and write a brief report (100 to 200 words). You are to describe the family who transmitted this heritage. Some questions are provided to guide your investigation.

1. In what time period did they live?

2. Describe the people who used these artifacts?

3. Where did these people live?

4. What impact did these people have on society (then and now)? What impact might these people have on the future? Support your conclusions.

5. Describe their family practices? What kind of problem solving approach (es) did they follow?

6. What evidence gives you information about their health, economic, political, religious, educational, or social status?

7. What impact on the land did these people make?

8. (other questions)

INSIDER VERSUS OUTSIDER OPINIONS
Ruth Burgess, © 1999

Reflection and tasks:

1. After reading the two narratives ("That Heritage Box" and "My Heritage Box") and reflecting on the contents, develop a comparative chart about the two approaches, write the criterion in the left column, and the descriptors in the remaining two columns.

2. At the bottom of the page write what you learned through this exercise. How can you apply this in the future when you work with families who have children with disabilities?

Criteria	That Heritage Box	My Heritage Box
1.		
2.		
3.		
4.		

From this experience I learned ...

Reflections on the Heritage Box Exercise
Ruth Burgess. © 1999

Reflect on the Heritage Box exercise. What understandings did you derive from this experience in the following areas?

1. (knowledge of fore-bearers)
2. (sense of self-identity)
3. (sense of group identity)
4. (building classroom understanding and community spirit)
5. (developing an understanding outside of the present time and place)
6. (Organization of time, space, people, events, values, use of errors...)
7. (intergenerational transmission continuity)
8. (beliefs in positive alterative/s)
9. (access to resources)
10. (role/s of children)
11. (your choice:)
12. (your choice:)

How can you use these insights to better understand and work with families who have exceptional family members? Write three sentences explaining your insights.

1.

2.

3.

Name:

Date:

INSIDER VERSUS OUTSIDER OPINIONS
Ruth Burgess. © 1999

Reflection on tasks:

1. After reading the two narratives ("That Heritage Box" and "My Heritage Box") and reflecting on the contents, develop a comparative chart about the two approaches, write the criterion in the left column, and the descriptors in the remaining two columns.

2. At the bottom of the page write what you learned through this exercise. How can you apply this in the future?

Criteria	(Outsider Viewpoint) **That Heritage Box**	(Insider Viewpoint) **My Heritage Box**
1. Thoroughness (number & types)		
2. Accuracy of interpretation of artifacts		
3. Appropriate interpretation of family's values & impact		
4. Value or worth of the artifacts		

From this experience I learned ...

Heritage Box Organization

Dr. Ruth Burgess. © 2005

Time related	**Space / location**
Religion	**Economics**
Politics	**Job / work**
War / peace	**Communication**
Rituals	**Food**
Oral tradition	**Order in family**
Clothing	**Entertainment**
Jewelry	**Sports**
Lodging	**Education:**
Other:	**Other:**

Contrasting Perspectives

My Heritage Box | That Heritage Box

The artifacts I chose were but a few from my maternal grandmother. It was hard to choose these artifacts tell the most about part of my family history.

The people lived in the 1900's. They were a traditional family, with a wedding and photos. They may have owned a family business with ledgers and notes. There was a reference to a corner store.

My brother and I called our grandmother "Nanmama." Her stories tell about her life in Nebraska and marriage to Grandpa.

The family tree was helpful for their future descendants. On a business trip to Texas they bought a calendar plate.

I learned my family fought in both the Civil War and Revolutionary War.

I think the wedding invitation represents a close knit family. Why were their several envelopes with different addresses?

Heritage Box Contents

1 Gaelic Bible | 1 book of songs written by grandmother
1 leather collar box | ancestor wearing a kilt
1 calculator | pictures 1900s
1 family tree | 1 black, leather coin purse

Students Reflections on the Exercise

Several weeks later the students wrote reflection papers relating to the Heritage Box experience. Several students' comments addressed several of the mediated learning parameters. Ten categories are presented below.

1. Knowledge of fore bearers

Student 1: "I found everyone in my family has a story to tell. I have a story to tell about everyone my family. Future generations rely on family member to pass on their knowledge of the past."

Student 2: "I learned about my grandmother's family members through the family friendship quilt. I now feel I am lacking in my knowledge of my other heritage."

Student 3: "I learned that my family is proud of who we are, but we don't really share stories about it."

2. Sense of self identity

Student 1: "I am a separate person than the rest of my family. I am not like one single person in my family. I have my own aspects and stories to pass on to future generations."

Student 2: "I learned a little about where I came from. Now I am interested in learning more."

Student 3: "It made me aware of my uniqueness in the family. While all of my siblings are different, I know my specialty."

3. Sense of group identity

Student 1: I understand now that I do relate to members of my family. There are aspects of me that are comparable to aspects of other family members. For example, I realized I have the same thirst for creativity as my Grandma Scott did."

Student 2: "I found there were several other classmates whose Italian backgrounds were similar to mine."

Student 3: "Group identity is developed through similar values and upbringing."

4. Building classroom understanding and community spirit

Student 1: "An activity such as the Heritage Box can create an understanding of different family backgrounds and cultures. It can create a sense of community inside the classroom to realize that everyone's family is different or similar in some ways."

Student 2: "It was great to see everyone was interested in me."

Student 3: "We are not all that different. There are things we share in common."

5. **Developing an understanding outside of the present time and place**

Student 1: "It was interesting to see how values and experiences were different from one another."

Student 2; "Many families had to struggle to get to where their family is today."

Student 3: "It reminded me of how important it is to learn, save and carry on my family's heritage."

6. **Organization of time, space, people, events, values, use of errors**

Student 1: "Organization was the hardest aspect of the Heritage Box exercise. My box had very little organization because I had objects to represent random people in my family. The people who organized their box around a central theme were able to portray the best view of their family."

Student 2: Many of the presenters had the same values as my family. Many of our predecessors have made mistakes or errors. We have learned from them and to avoid them."

Student 3: "By organizing our family's values, we better understand them."

7. **Intergenerational continuities**

Student 1: "It is important to save artifacts to pass on to future generations so your story can be passed on as well. I am a visual learner and tend to remember stories best if they have a visual to accompany them. I wish my family had saved more visual stories.

Student 2: "My family did not pass down many artifacts. They passed down stories and ideas."

Student 3: "We are part of a community and we love that. But we are family first."

8. Belief in positive alternatives

Student 1: "Through this exercise I found that my family has consistently looked for ways they could better themselves. I think the struggle during the hard times helped our family to be strong through the other years."

Student 2: "Families must learn from past successes and failures. They must look at events on a case by case basis."

Student 3: No response

9. Access to Resources

Student 1: "Not all families have access to family artifacts. Some people may be cut off from certain sides of their family. Personally, I had a terrible time finding resources for my Heritage Box. This may be the case for many other people as well."

Student 2: "Historically, my family has really struggled to have resources to survive." Both sides went through very difficult times when they barely had enough to live. My dad commented that he didn't want us to go without like he did."

Student 3: "If a family does not have resources available, it is difficult to carry on the traditions."

10. Role of Children

Student 1: "Different families have different roles for children. Some children have the luxury of being able to play away their childhood while others have to begin working for the family at a young age."

Student 2: "In earlier times children worked on the farm in order to help the family survive."

Student 3: "The children are values as individuals on my Mom's side. On my Dad's side, it is the opposite. Children are expected to conform to parent's standards and society's standards."

Reflections on the Heritage Box Exercise
Ruth Burgess. © 1999

Reflect on the Heritage Box exercise. What understandings did you derive from this experience in the following areas?

1. (knowledge of fore-bearers)
2. (sense of self-identity)
3. (sense of group identity)
4. (building classroom understanding and community spirit)
5. (developing an understanding outside of the present time and place)
6. (organization of time, space, people, events, values, use of errors,...)
7. (intergenerational transmission continuity)
8. (beliefs in positive alterative/s)
9. (access to resources)
10. (role/s of children)
11. (your choice:)
12. (your choice:)

How can you use these insights to better understand and work with families who have exceptional family members? Write three sentences explaining your insights.

1.

2.

3.

Name _____ Date _____

Reflections on the Heritage Box Exercise
Students. © 2000

1. I have gained much insight into my family. I have learned nicknames, what jobs they participated in, how they lived, their personalities and interests. I also have gained inquisitiveness in following and researching this heritage more and to document my family information.

2. I feel that I am a stronger person in many ways. I feel that success can be attained. And that my definition of success has changed. I am more open to the future and have learned more about this past year since my perspectives have changed. I think that I have grown in some manner, but I'm still in the process of reflection.

3. I have learned much about the community I live in by participating in this project. Listening to the stories and looking at the artifact of other classmates has fostered understanding and empathy on my part.

4. Empathy has made me able to communicate with other classmates without feeling stifled. I feel that I am better able to respect their opinion of things. I think we are creating more of a caring classroom.

5. I have a greater understanding of how our past influences the future. Habits of the mind and habits of the heart have a foundation with how I was raised. Heritage is an influential part of who we are. It is important to reflect on this.

6. This project allows an element of choice for students. The artifacts chosen reflect the values of each participant. Through this selection process one may see differences in religion, values, geographic location, and citizenship.

7. There is definitely a stronger bond in this class. After not having class for two days last week, I felt reassured when we came back on Thursday. Seeing familiar faces during the storm was reassuring.

8. I definitely feel much more optimistic than before this exercise. I feel that my opinions about myself are stronger and that outside pressures have not impacted my self-confidence so negatively as they would a have in the past. I feel stronger in this regard.

9. I have found valuable information through my relatives. I have collected information by obtaining a genealogy book that has a wealth of information. I am also preserving old photographs by placing them in photo-friendly albums.

10. I definitely will use this project idea in my classroom. It is important to help foster a sense of heritage for children. I think that they can gain much insight into their own lives and their classmates' personalities. It's also a great way to get parents involved with school and their children.

Summary

Student relationships emerged and were strengthened through the Heritage Box Exercise. New and more in depth communication patterns were established cross generationally. Besides learning occupation and travel information, the students began to realize many of their forbearers learned skills in order to assist survival. Relocating families offered the promise of a better land and lifestyle. Barbara wrote, *"I, too, share the same spirit of seeking a better life, as I have always met new moves or relocations with much anticipation. I share many of the same values and spiritual beliefs as my ancestors."*

To address uncomfortable or awkward feeling the class adopted the

131

motto. *"There are no bad ideas created in this room!"* The students began to relate one to the other in sensitive ways as they learned the inadequacies of external observations. Interview styles replaced authoritative comments. They began to express the need to seek others' insight first, rather than judging them. Moving beyond how the artifact looked, the students moved to higher orders of thinking. Debbie wrote, *"I felt like a link in the chain of similarities and differences. I celebrate our differences and feel very close to other students."*

Sad sagas were told of neglected preservations of heritage stories and artifacts. Many wished that more information and additional artifacts could have been located. Through the encouragement and support of their classmates, each student emerged with the realization that they could become a culture bearer of their rich traditions. This urgency to assume this role came as students realized that individuals need to know their heritage so they won't seek self-identity elsewhere. Humans need both individual and group identities. As Angela summed up, *"Different artifacts and experiences are seen in many ways according to your culture, beliefs, standards and experiences."*

Supplement D

Extending Shantistan

These forms either supplement the Heritage Box exercise or assist in making alternative plans.

1. Critique Worksheet: this problem-solving exercise is to be completed before beginning a project.
2. Cultural Impressions: combines cross-cultural values and thinking skills
3. Dilemmas: group thinking while problem solving
4. K.W.D.L.Q.: Making plans for a long - term project, coordinate, adjust to combine the problem solving of others in order to attain harmony
5. Reconciliation: Cognitive. – Behavioral Reflections: negotiate using principles of mediated learning to reach an agreement.
6. *Without a Heritage,"* Carolyn B. Nixon, poem
7. Voices that Have Impacted Me, graphic

CRITIQUE WORKSHEET

1   **PURPOSE** OF THE EXERCISE

2   **THE THRAS** STATEMENT OR DESCRIPTION OF PROBLEM

3   **DEDUCING THE THRAS** CONCEPTS & ISSUES

4   **IDENTIFYING** EVALUATION STANDARDS OR CRITERIA

5   **FOCUS AND COMPARISON** HOW IS THE THRAS SIMILAR TO ANOTHER INCIDENT ELSEWHERE OR DURING ANOTHER TIME PERIOD?

6 **POSSIBLE SHORT-TERM EFFECTS** IF ALLOWED TO CONTINUE

7 **POSSIBLE LONG-TERM EFFECTS** IF ALLOWED TO CONTINUE

8 **FOCUSED FINDINGS** WHAT MIGHT BE THE BEST PLAN TO FOLLOW?

CULTURAL IMPRESSIONS

Instructions: After completing your heritage story, first write your values in Column A. In Column B, Write how another culture perceives your heritage value. In Column C, explain in what manner your culture displays that value. After thinking, decide if you plan to transmit this value or virtue in to the future. Write your thoughts in column D.

A	B	C	D
My Heritage Values are listed below.	Another Culture's Values	How my Culture Displays These Values	Should I Transmit these values in the future?
1.			
2.			
3.			
4.			
5.			

Comments:

DILEMMAS...

(Greek "involving at least two assumptions")

Ruth Burgess, ©1996

A POTENTIAL FOR DEVELOPING UNDERSTANDING

I.   Read "the equitable solution dilemma"

II. Discuss the dilemma, propose assumptions made by the persons, involved.

A.	**B.**
ASSUMPTIONS	**ASSUMPTIONS**

III. Analyze the logic behind the assumption.

IV. Write the problem in less than four sentences.

V. Define equity, define just, define honorable, how do these three concepts apply to the solution of this problem?

		Topic of Inquiry		
K What We **K**now	**W** What We **W**ant toKnow	**D** By What **D**ate	**L** What We **L**earned	**Q** Further **Q**uestions

Resources we will need to accomplish this inquiry:

K, W, D, L, Q, Burgess, 2001

Reconciliation: Cognitive – Behavioral Reflections (2004)

1. **Situation:** (e.g. Describe a conflict that stimulates the need to confront, …)	2. **Perception or Inner Dialogue:** (e.g. I don't want him to hurt. …)
3. **Emotional Response:** (e.g. anger, fear, love…)	4. **Behavioral Response:** (e.g. Withdrawal, …)
5. **Physiological Effect:** (e.g. increased headaches, stomach, pain, …)	6. **Logical Insights and Evaluation of the Process:** (e.g. "Good mediators seek meaning within boundaries." …)
7. **Bridging:** (In what ways can I apply these insights to bring reconciliation?	
8. **Other Comments:**	

Voices That Have Impacted Me

© Ruth Burgess 1990

What was imparted? Who imparted it? How did they impart it?

Without A Heritage

An empty box
A bottomless hole
An endless ache

Memories –
Gone like the wind
Blowing softly
Then gusting away
Into the endless abyss of Time

Memories –
Capture the wind
Softly encase it.
Save it for the Future,
The endless abyss of Time.

© Carolyn B. Nixon, 1992

GLOSSARY OF SELECTED VOCABULARY

Alloplastic: a person controlled by and attributing causation to outside forces (external locus of control)

Autoplastic: a person reflects through metacognition and reasoned dispositions of the mind, one who takes responsibility for his thoughts and actions (Internal locus of control)

Co-cultures: a term that signifies that more than one culture exists and both share similar complementary spatial plans, but may have different heritages

Cognitive modifiability: "an approach that is not directed at the remediation of specific behaviors and skills but at changes of a structural nature that alter the course and direction of cognitive behavior." (R. Feuerstein et al, 2006, p.16) An individual's propensity to be changed by direct and mediated learning experiences.

Culture: the social and individual modes of thinking, organized data, educing relationships and using heritage, contemporary and scientific way to manage society

Culture bearer: individuals who treasure and promote active use of historical and heritage artifacts, sites and narratives

Cultural deprivation: one who is internally alienated from their culture such as disruption of intergenerational transmission

Ethnologic: one's way of thinking based on a cultural logic

Heritage: one's cultural entitlements transmitted from prior generations

Life experience narrative: stories based on life experiences

Mediated learning experience (MLE): the formula for a MLE is Stimulus-Human Organism-Human-Response. Three elements are present: intent and reciprocity, search for meaning, educe transcendent values or wisdom principles

Mediatee: the child or adult who is the recipient of mediation

Mediator: a person who treasures heritage habits of the mind and habit of the spirit, he is willing to be an intergenerational culture bearer of those values and wisdom principles

Metacognition: to reflect on one's thinking

Multiple perspectives: different cultural perceptions or thoughts relating to meanings, concepts, situations, issues or logics

Metapraxis: to reflect on the process of one's thinking

Peace: when individuals or groups are untroubled, they work to prevent or avoid strife

Peace themes: Ideas that promote calm, not given to dispute, promote friendly relations

Problem Solving: different approaches attempting to solve cognitive or social dissonance

Process: the "how" by which the person processes, reflects and formulates

Product: the end result of some actions or effort

Shantistan: a transcultural curriculum committed to building peace

Theory of Structural Cognitive Modifiability (structural change): advocates that brain structures may change as a result of mediated learning experiences.The three integral factors include (1) changes in the parts to the whole, (2) transformations occur in the context of change, and (3) self-perpetuation of changes occur within the cognitive schemata.

Use: how communication acts are used in different contexts

Values: something of worth to culture or ethnic group, beliefs that determine a person's thinking, actions and character

Vertical orientation: relates to levels of abstraction and complexity when a mediator is mediating higher levels of thought

Transcendent values: abstract values or wisdom principles that extend beyond usual limits, surpassing usual information These extend beyond person, place, time and circumstances.

Wisdom principles: intergenerational values that initially were part of the groups' oral history and later were codified, the group or tribe may consider these as transcendent sayings

Zone of Proximal Development: the phase at which a person can master a task if given appropriate help and support. The space (zone) between an assisted and an unassisted performance.

ACKNOWLEDGEMENTS

The author gratefully acknowledges permission to quote briefly material from the following family and friends.

Matthew, Scott and David Burgess who gave love and assistance to the disposed in foreign lands. (1985)

Bradley Burgess who graciously shared his photography arts and kindness. (1984)

Sophia Burgess for sharing her graphic arts. (2020)

Edward Chang who nurtured cross-generational vitality. (1991)

Elizabeth Dotson for creating visuals for the Shantistan Quilt. (2019)

Mr. Bhatt, Dolly Bhat, Roma Rajan, Henry Christian, Mr. Saikh and Shabana who expedited the field testing in India. (1995)

Robbie Kargarise for sharing Regent University classroom experience stories that were used cross-culturally. (2008)

Amanda Levinson who shared gentle social dispositions of the spirit abroad. (1986)

Karl Luckert for his cross-culture definition of religion. (2009)

Liang Yi Lin supported the belief of global bonds. (1991)

Carolyn Brown Nixon's poems produce a yearning for heritage memories. (1992)

Doug and Lois Olena's support for multiple perspectives. (2018)

Michael Palmer's respect for children's insights. (2003)

My students who traveled with me down "roads called heritage find and mediated learning." (1999)

Mark Richardson for the use of his poem, *Listening Here.* (1991)

Jacqueline Schlesinger, a friend who gives honest feedback and provides thoughtful kindness. (2010)

Mark Shipley for his astute videography and thoughtfulness. (2017)

Helen Sullivan who cares for peace and justice across cultural barriers. (1995)

Richard Turner insights concerning "Appreciating for Positive Disequilibrium." (1991)

Kory Waschick for being a graphic artist who illustrated concepts and human experiences well. (2020)

BIBLIOGRAPHY

Brosh, Na'ama & Rachel Milstain. 1992. *Biblical stories in Islamic Painting.* Jerusalem, Israel: The Israel Museum.

Burgess, Ruth & J. David Burgess. 2015. *Longing for Home.* Indiana: Xlibris Press.

Burgess, Ruth 2008. *Changing Brain Structure Through Cross-Cultural learning, The Life of Reuven Feuerstein.* Lewiston: The Edwin Mellen Press.

Clemens, Thoma & Michel Wyschogrod. 1989. *Parable & Story in Judaism & Christianity.* New Jersey: Paulist Press.

Feuerstein, Reuven, Louis Falik & Rafael Feuerstein 2015. *Changing Minds & Brains - the Legacy of Reuven Feuerstein. Higher Thinking & Cognition Through Meditated Learning.* New York: Teacher College Press. Columbia, University

Feuerstein Shmuel. 2002. *Biblical & Talmudic Antecedents of Mediated Learning Experience Theory. Educational and Didactic Implications for Inter-Generational Cultural Transmission.* Jerusalem, Israel: The International Center for the Enhancement of Learning Potential Press.

George, Emery, ed. 1993. *Contemporary East European Poetry, an Anthology.* London: Oxford University Press

Kimbell-Lopez, Kimberly. 1999. *Connecting with Traditional Literature.* Needham Heights, MA: Allyn & Bacon

Newberg, Eric N. & Lois E. Olena. 2014. *Children of the Calling. Essays in Honor of Stanley M. Burgess & Ruth V. Burgess.* Eugene, Oregon: Pickwick Publications.

Newbigin. Lesslie. 1986. *Foolishness to the Greeks, The Gospel and Western Culture.* Cambridge, U.K.: William B. Eerdmans Publishing Company.

Purves, Alan C. 1988. *Writing Across Language and Cultures. Issues in Contrastive Rhetoric.* New Delhi: Sage Publications.

Washburn, Phil. 1997. *Philosophical Dilemmas. Building a Worldview.* New York: Oxford University Press

Wertheimer, Jack eds. 1992. *The Uses of Tradition. Jewish Continuity in the Modern Era.* New York and Jerusalem. London: Harvard University Press.

Winternitz, Moriz. 1996. *A History of Indian Literature, Volume 1.* India: Motilal Banarsidass Publ.

Young, Robert. 1990. *A Critical Theory of Education.* New York: Teacher's College, Columbia University Press.

Shantistan
Inspired by
Stan & Ruth Burgess
Made by
Elizabeth Dotson
2019

Printed in the United States
By Bookmasters

Printed in the United States
By Bookmasters